Instant Pot®
FAVORITES

Publications International, Ltd.

CONTENTS

INTRODUCTION

Welcome to the wonderful world of Instant Pot cooking!

Although the current craze makes it seem like a new invention, pressure cooking has actually been around for a few hundred years. Many people grew up hearing stories of pressure cooker catastrophes—exploding pots and soup on the ceiling—but those days are long gone. There have been great changes and improvements in recent years to make modern pressure cookers completely safe, quiet and easy to use.

What exactly is a pressure cooker?

It's a simple concept: Liquid is heated in a heavy pot with a lid that locks and forms an airtight seal. Since the steam from the hot liquid is trapped inside and can't evaporate, the pressure increases and raises the boiling point of the contents in the pot, and these items cook faster at a higher temperature. In general, pressure cooking can reduce cooking time to about one third of the time used in conventional cooking methods—and typically the time spent on pressure cooking is hands off. (There's no peeking or stirring when food is being cooked under pressure.)

What makes the Instant Pot different?

The Instant Pot is a versatile electric multi-cooker that can be a pressure cooker, rice cooker, slow cooker, steamer and yogurt maker. The cooking programs you'll find on the control panel are convenient shortcuts for some foods you may prepare regularly (rice, beans, etc.) which use preset times and cooking levels. But in these pages we'll explore the basics of pressure cooking with recipes that primarily use the Manual or Pressure Cook button along with customized cooking times and pressure levels. These simple and delicious dishes will inspire you to use your Instant Pot® daily and create your own Instant Pot magic!

Butter Chicken, *page 112*

Chunky Ranch Potatoes, *page 204*

Instant Pot Components

The **exterior pot** is where the electrical components are housed. It should never be immersed in water; to clean it, simply unplug the unit, wipe it with a damp cloth and dry it immediately.

The **inner pot** holds the food and fits snugly into the exterior pot. Made of stainless steel, it is removable, and it can be washed by hand or in the dishwasher.

The **LED display** shows a time that indicates where the pressure cooker is in a particular function. The time counts down to zero from the number of minutes that were programmed. (The timing begins once the machine reaches pressure.) For Keep Warm and Yogurt functions, the time counts up.

The **pressure release valve** is on top of the lid and is used to seal the pot or release steam. To seal the pot, move the valve to the Sealing position; to release pressure, move the valve to the Venting position. This valve can pop off to clean, and to make sure nothing is blocking it.

The **float valve** controls the amount of pressure inside the pressure cooker and indicates when pressure cooking is taking place. The valve rises once the contents of the pot reach working pressure; it drops down when all the pressure has been released after cooking.

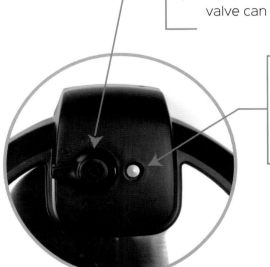

The **anti-block shield** is a small stainless steel cage found on the inside of the lid that prevents the pressure cooker from clogging. It can be removed for cleaning.

The **silicone sealing ring** underneath the lid helps create a tight seal to facilitate pressure cooking. The sealing ring has a tendency to absorb strong odors from cooking (particularly from acidic ingredients); washing it regularly with warm soapy water or in the dishwasher will help these odors dissipate, as will storing your Instant Pot® with the lid ring side up. If you cook both sweet and savory dishes frequently, you may want to purchase an extra sealing ring (so the scent of curry or pot roast doesn't affect your rice pudding or crème brûlée). Make sure to inspect the ring before cooking—if it has any splits or cracks, it will not work properly and should be replaced.

Instant Pot Cooking Basics

Every recipe is slightly different, but most include these basic steps. Read through the entire recipe before beginning to cook so you'll know what ingredients to add and when to add them, which pressure level to use, the cooking time and the release method.

1. Sauté: Many recipes call for sautéing vegetables or browning meat at the beginning of a recipe to add flavor. (Be sure to leave the lid off in this step.)

2. Add the ingredients as the recipe directs and secure the lid, making sure the arrow mark on the lid is aligned with the "close" mark and lock icon on the rim of the outside pot. Turn the pressure release valve to the Sealing position.

3. Select Pressure Cook or Manual, then choose the pressure level. The default setting is high pressure, which is what most recipes in this book use. To change to low pressure, use the Adjust or Pressure Level button. To set the cooking time, use the + and - buttons. The Instant Pot will start automatically.

4. Once the pressure cooking is complete, use the pressure release method directed by the recipe. There are three types of releases:

Natural release:

Let the pressure slowly release on its own, which can take anywhere from 5 to 25 minutes (but is typically in the 10- to 15-minute range). The release time will be shorter for a pot that is less full and longer for one that is more full. When the float valve lowers, the pressure is released and you can open the lid.

Quick release:

Use a towel or pot holder to manually turn the pressure valve to the Venting position immediately after the cooking is complete. (Be sure to get out of the way of the steam before turning the valve.) It can take up to 2 minutes to fully release all the pressure; the float valve will drop down when all the pressure is released.

A combination of natural and quick release:

The recipe will instruct you to let the pressure release naturally for a certain amount of time (frequently for 10 minutes), and then do a quick release as directed.

Tips, Tricks, Dos and Don'ts

- Read the manual before beginning. There may be features you won't use, but it will eliminate some beginner's confusion, and it can help you understand how the Instant Pot works—and see all its possibilities. Models also change over time, so the manual can provide the best information about the buttons and functions of your pot. (Note that the terms "Pressure Cook" and "Manual" are interchangeable.)

- Don't overfill the pot—the total amount of food and liquid should not exceed the maximum level marked on the inner pot. Generally it is best not to fill the pot more than two thirds full; when cooking foods that expand during cooking such as beans and grains, do not fill it more than half full.

- Make sure there is always some liquid in the pot before cooking because a minimum amount is required to come up to pressure (the amount differs between models). However, if the recipe contains a large quantity of vegetables or meats, you may be able to use a bit less since these ingredients will create their own liquid.

- Always check that the pressure release valve is in the right position before you start pressure cooking. The food simply won't get cooked if the valve is not in the Sealing position because there will not be enough pressure in the pot.

- Never try to force the lid open after cooking—if the lid won't open, that means the pressure has not fully released. (As a safety feature, the lid remains locked until the float valve drops down.)

- Save the thickeners for after the pressure cooking is done. Pressure cooker recipes often end up with a lot of flavorful liquid left in the pot when cooking is complete; flour or cornstarch mixtures can thicken these liquids into delicious sauces. Use the Sauté function while incorporating the thickeners into the cooking liquid, and then cook and stir until the desired consistency is reached.

- Keep in mind that cooking times in some recipes may vary. We've included pressure cooking time charts as a guide (pages 248–251), but these are approximate times, and numerous variables may cause your results to be different. For example, the freshness of dried beans affects their cooking time (older beans take longer to cook), as does what they are cooked with—hard water (water that is high in mineral content), acidic ingredients, sugar and salt levels can also affect cooking times. So be flexible and experiment with what works best for you—you can always check the doneness of your food and add more time.

- Set reasonable expectations, i.e., don't expect everything you cook in the Instant Pot to be ready in a few minutes. Even though it reduces many conventional cooking times dramatically, nothing is literally "instant"—it will always take time to get up to pressure, and then to release it. (These machines are fast but not magical!)

GRAINS & BEANS

White Beans and Tomatoes

Makes 8 to 10 servings

1 pound dried cannellini beans, soaked 8 hours or overnight

2 tablespoons olive oil

2 medium onions, chopped

1 tablespoon minced garlic

1 tablespoon tomato paste

4 teaspoons dried oregano

2 teaspoons salt

1 can (28 ounces) crushed tomatoes

2 cups water

Black pepper (optional)

1 Drain and rinse beans. Press Sauté; heat oil in Instant Pot. Add onions; cook and stir 5 to 7 minutes or until tender and lightly browned.

2 Add garlic, tomato paste, oregano and salt; cook and stir 1 minute. Stir in beans, tomatoes and water; mix well.

3 Secure lid and move pressure release valve to Sealing position. Press Pressure Cook or Manual; cook at high pressure 16 minutes.

4 When cooking is complete, use natural release for 10 minutes, then release remaining pressure. Season with black pepper, if desired.

Creamy Barley Risotto

Makes 4 servings

- 1 tablespoon olive oil
- 1 large leek, halved and thinly sliced
- 1 cup uncooked pearled barley
- 1 teaspoon salt
- 2 cups vegetable broth
- 1/4 teaspoon black pepper
- 1 cup frozen peas
- 1/2 cup shredded Parmesan cheese
- 2 tablespoons butter, cut into pieces
- 1 tablespoon lemon juice
- 1 teaspoon grated lemon peel, plus additional for garnish
- Shaved Parmesan cheese (optional)
- Chopped fresh Italian parsley (optional)

1 Press Sauté; heat oil in Instant Pot. Add leek; cook and stir 3 minutes or until softened and beginning to lightly brown. Add barley and salt; cook and stir 1 minute. Stir in broth and pepper; mix well.

2 Secure lid and move pressure release valve to Sealing position. Press Pressure Cook or Manual; cook at high pressure 18 minutes.

3 When cooking is complete, use natural release for 10 minutes, then release remaining pressure.

4 Stir in peas, 1/2 cup shredded cheese, butter, lemon juice and 1 teaspoon lemon peel. Garnish with shaved cheese, additional lemon peel and parsley.

Cheesy Polenta

Makes 6 servings

5 cups vegetable broth

½ teaspoon salt

1½ cups uncooked instant polenta

½ cup grated Parmesan cheese

¼ cup (½ stick) butter, cubed, plus additional for serving

Fried sage leaves (optional)

1 Combine broth and salt in Instant Pot; slowly whisk in polenta until blended.

2 Secure lid and move pressure release valve to Sealing position. Press Pressure Cook or Manual; cook at high pressure 5 minutes.

3 When cooking is complete, use natural release for 5 minutes, then release remaining pressure.

4 Whisk in cheese and ¼ cup butter until well blended. (Polenta may appear separated immediately after cooking but will come together when stirred.) Serve with additional butter; garnish with sage.

Tip

Spread any leftover polenta in a baking dish and refrigerate until cold. Cut the cold polenta into sticks or slices, brush with olive oil and pan-fry or grill until lightly browned.

Note

Chicken broth may be substituted for vegetable broth. Or use water and add an additional ½ teaspoon salt when whisking in the polenta.

Pesto Rice and Beans

Makes 4 servings

½ cup dried Great Northern beans, soaked 8 hours or overnight

1½ cups water or chicken broth, divided

¼ teaspoon salt, divided

½ cup uncooked long grain rice

4 ounces fresh green beans, cut into 1-inch pieces (about ¾ cup)

¼ cup prepared pesto

Shredded Parmesan cheese, chopped plum tomatoes and chopped fresh parsley (optional)

1 Drain and rinse Great Northern beans. Combine beans, 1 cup water and ⅛ teaspoon salt in Instant Pot; mix well. Secure lid and move pressure release valve to Sealing position. Press Manual; cook at high pressure 4 minutes.

2 Meanwhile, rinse rice well; drain in fine-mesh strainer. Combine rice, remaining ½ cup water and ⅛ teaspoon salt in small metal or ceramic bowl that fits inside pot; mix well. Place green beans in center of 12-inch square of foil; sprinkle with additional salt. Bring up two sides of foil over beans; fold foil over several times to create packet. Fold in opposite ends. (Packet should measure about 8×4 inches.)

3 When cooking of Great Northern beans is complete, press Cancel and use quick release. Place bowl with rice on rack; lower rack into pot. Arrange foil packet on top of bowl. (Packet should not entirely cover bowl.) Secure lid and move pressure release valve to Sealing position. Press Pressure Cook or Manual; cook at high pressure 4 minutes.

4 When cooking is complete, use natural release for 8 minutes, then release remaining pressure. Use handles of rack to remove bowl and foil packet from pot. If any liquid remains in bottom of pot with Great Northern beans, press Sauté; cook 1 to 2 minutes or until liquid is evaporated.

5 Add Great Northern beans and green beans to bowl with rice; gently stir in pesto. Top with cheese, tomatoes and parsley, if desired.

Farro Risotto with Mushrooms and Spinach

Makes 4 servings

2 tablespoons olive oil, divided

1 onion, chopped

12 ounces cremini mushrooms, trimmed and quartered

1 teaspoon salt

¼ teaspoon black pepper

2 cloves garlic, minced

1 cup uncooked pearled farro

1 sprig fresh thyme

1½ cups vegetable or chicken broth

1 package (5 to 6 ounces) baby spinach

½ cup grated Parmesan cheese

1 Press Sauté; heat 1 tablespoon oil in Instant Pot. Add onion; cook and stir 5 minutes or until translucent. Add remaining 1 tablespoon oil, mushrooms, salt and pepper; cook about 8 minutes or until mushrooms have released their liquid and are browned, stirring occasionally. Add garlic; cook and stir 1 minute. Add farro and thyme; cook and stir 1 minute. Add broth; mix well.

2 Secure lid and move pressure release valve to Sealing position. Press Pressure Cook or Manual; cook at high pressure 10 minutes.

3 When cooking is complete, use natural release for 10 minutes, then release remaining pressure. Remove and discard thyme sprig.

4 Stir in spinach and cheese until spinach is wilted.

Four-Bean Chili Stew

Makes 6 servings

¾ cup dried kidney beans

¾ cup dried chickpeas

¾ cup dried Great Northern beans

¾ cup dried black beans

2 cans (about 11 ounces each) tomatillos, drained

1 can (about 15 ounces) tomato sauce

1½ cups water

1 cup prepared barbecue sauce

1 onion, chopped

3 cloves garlic, minced

1½ teaspoons ground cumin

1½ teaspoons chili powder

½ teaspoon salt

¼ teaspoon ground red pepper

1 zucchini, halved lengthwise, then cut crosswise into 1-inch slices

½ red bell pepper, chopped

Flour tortillas, warmed (optional)

Optional toppings: sour cream, chopped tomato, chopped onion, shredded Cheddar cheese, chopped fresh cilantro (optional)

1 Rinse beans separately in colander under cold water, picking out any debris or blemished beans. Combine kidney beans, chickpeas and Great Northern beans in large bowl; cover with water. Place black beans in medium bowl; cover with water.* Soak 8 hours or overnight.

2 Drain and rinse all beans. Place in Instant Pot with tomatillos, tomato sauce, 1½ cups water, barbecue sauce, onion, garlic, cumin, chili powder, salt and ground red pepper; mix well.

3 Secure lid and move pressure release valve to Sealing position. Press Pressure Cook or Manual; cook at high pressure 20 minutes.

4 When cooking is complete, use natural release for 5 minutes, then release remaining pressure.

5 Stir in zucchini and bell pepper. Secure lid and move pressure release valve to Sealing position. Press Pressure Cook or Manual; cook at high pressure 1 minute. When cooking is complete, press Cancel and use quick release. Serve with tortillas and desired garnishes.

Soaking black beans with the other beans will turn the Great Northerns and chickpeas purple.

Classic Irish Oatmeal

Makes 4 servings

2 tablespoons butter

1 cup steel-cut oats

3 cups water

½ teaspoon salt

½ teaspoon ground cinnamon

Berry Compote (recipe follows, optional)

⅓ cup half-and-half

¼ cup packed brown sugar

1 Press Sauté; melt butter in Instant Pot. Add oats; cook about 6 minutes, stirring frequently. Add water, salt and cinnamon; cook and stir 1 minute.

2 Secure lid and move pressure release valve to Sealing position. Press Pressure Cook or Manual; cook at high pressure 13 minutes. Meanwhile, prepare Berry Compote, if desired.

3 When cooking is complete, press Cancel to turn off heat. Use natural release for 10 minutes, then release remaining pressure.

4 Stir oats until smooth. Add half-and-half and brown sugar; stir until well blended. If thicker porridge is desired, press Sauté and cook 2 to 3 minutes or until desired thickness, stirring constantly. (Porridge will also thicken upon standing.) Serve with Berry Compote.

Berry Compote

Combine 1 cup quartered fresh strawberries, 6 ounces fresh blackberries, 6 ounces fresh blueberries, 3 tablespoons granulated sugar and 1 tablespoon water in medium saucepan; bring to a simmer over medium heat. Cook 8 to 9 minutes or until berries are tender but still hold their shape, stirring occasionally.

Spinach Risotto

Makes 4 servings

- 2 tablespoons olive oil
- 2 tablespoons butter, divided
- 1 shallot, finely chopped
- 1½ cups uncooked arborio rice
- 1½ teaspoons salt
- ¼ teaspoon black pepper
- ½ cup dry white wine
- 4 cups vegetable broth
- 2 cups packed baby spinach
- ½ cup shredded Parmesan cheese
- 2 tablespoons pine nuts, toasted*

To toast pine nuts, cook in small skillet over medium heat 3 minutes or until lightly browned, stirring frequently.

1 Press Sauté; heat oil and 1 tablespoon butter in Instant Pot. Add shallot; cook and stir 2 minutes or until softened. Add rice; cook and stir 3 minutes or until rice is translucent. Stir in salt and pepper. Add wine; cook and stir about 1 minute or until evaporated. Stir in broth; mix well.

2 Secure lid and move pressure release valve to Sealing position. Press Pressure Cook or Manual; cook at high pressure 6 minutes.

3 When cooking is complete, press Cancel and use quick release.

4 Press Sauté; adjust heat to low ("less"). Add spinach to pot; cook about 3 minutes or until spinach is wilted and risotto reaches desired consistency, stirring constantly. Stir in cheese and remaining 1 tablespoon butter until blended. Sprinkle with pine nuts.

Chickpea Tikka Masala

Makes 4 servings

1¼ cups dried chickpeas, soaked 8 hours or overnight

1 tablespoon olive oil

1 onion, chopped

3 cloves garlic, minced

1 tablespoon minced fresh ginger or ginger paste

1 tablespoon garam masala

1½ teaspoons salt

1 teaspoon ground coriander

1 teaspoon ground cumin

¼ teaspoon ground red pepper

1 can (28 ounces) crushed tomatoes

1 can (about 13 ounces) coconut milk

1 package (about 12 ounces) paneer cheese, cut into 1-inch cubes

Hot cooked basmati rice (optional)

Chopped fresh cilantro

1 Drain and rinse chickpeas. Press Sauté; heat oil in Instant Pot. Add onion; cook and stir 5 minutes or until translucent. Add garlic, ginger, garam masala, salt, coriander, cumin and red pepper; cook and stir 1 minute. Stir in chickpeas, tomatoes and coconut milk; mix well.

2 Secure lid and move pressure release valve to Sealing position. Press Pressure Cook or Manual; cook at high pressure 22 minutes.

3 When cooking is complete, use natural release for 10 minutes, then release remaining pressure.

4 Press Sauté; adjust heat to low ("less"). Add paneer to pot; stir gently. Cook 5 minutes or until paneer is heated through, stirring occasionally. Serve with rice, if desired; sprinkle with cilantro.

Variation

For a vegan dish, substitute one package (about 12 ounces) firm silken tofu, drained and cut into 1-inch cubes, for the paneer.

Barley with Currants and Pine Nuts

Makes 4 to 6 servings

2 tablespoons butter

1 onion, finely chopped

2 cups vegetable broth

1 cup uncooked pearled barley

½ cup currants

½ teaspoon salt

¼ teaspoon black pepper

2 ounces (about ½ cup) pine nuts, toasted*

To toast pine nuts, cook in small skillet over medium heat 3 minutes or until lightly browned, stirring frequently.

1 Press Sauté; melt butter in Instant Pot. Add onion; cook and stir 5 minutes or until tender. Stir in broth, barley, currants, salt and pepper; mix well.

2 Secure lid and move pressure release valve to Sealing position. Press Pressure Cook or Manual; cook at high pressure 18 minutes.

3 When cooking is complete, use natural release for 10 minutes, then release remaining pressure.

4 Stir in pine nuts. Serve warm or at room temperature.

Winter Squash Risotto

Makes 4 to 6 servings

- 2 tablespoons butter
- 1 tablespoon olive oil
- 1 large shallot or small onion, finely chopped
- 1½ cups uncooked arborio rice
- 1 teaspoon salt
- ½ teaspoon dried thyme
- ¼ teaspoon black pepper
- ¼ cup dry white wine
- 4 cups vegetable or chicken broth
- 2 cups cubed butternut squash (½-inch pieces)
- ½ grated Parmesan or Romano cheese, plus additional for garnish

1 Press Sauté; heat butter and oil in Instant Pot. Add shallot; cook and stir 2 minutes or until softened. Add rice; cook and stir 4 minutes or until rice is translucent. Stir in salt, thyme and pepper. Add wine; cook and stir about 1 minute or until evaporated. Add broth and squash; mix well.

2 Secure lid and move pressure release valve to Sealing position. Press Pressure Cook or Manual; cook at high pressure 6 minutes.

3 When cooking is complete, press Cancel and use quick release.

4 Press Sauté; adjust heat to low ("less"). Cook risotto about 3 minutes or until desired consistency, stirring constantly. Stir in ½ cup cheese. Serve immediately with additional cheese.

Vegetarian Chili

Makes 8 to 10 servings

2 tablespoons olive oil

1 onion, finely chopped

2 medium carrots, chopped

1 red bell pepper, chopped

3 tablespoons chili powder

2 tablespoons tomato paste

2 tablespoons packed dark brown sugar

2 tablespoons ground cumin

3 cloves garlic, minced

1 tablespoon dried oregano

2 teaspoons salt

1 can (28 ounces) diced tomatoes

1 can (15 ounces) tomato sauce

1 can (about 15 ounces) small white beans, rinsed and drained

1 can (about 15 ounces) light kidney beans, rinsed and drained

1 can (about 15 ounces) dark kidney beans, rinsed and drained

1 can (about 15 ounces) pinto beans, rinsed and drained

1 can (4 ounces) diced green chiles

1 ounce unsweetened chocolate, chopped

1 tablespoon cider vinegar

1 Press Sauté; heat oil in Instant Pot. Add onion, carrots and bell pepper; cook and stir 5 minutes or until vegetables are softened.

2 Add chili powder, tomato paste, brown sugar, cumin, garlic, oregano and salt; cook and stir 1 minute. Stir in tomatoes, tomato sauce, beans and chiles; mix well.

3 Secure lid and move pressure release valve to Sealing position. Press Pressure Cook or Manual; cook at high pressure 10 minutes.

4 When cooking is complete, use natural release for 10 minutes, then release remaining pressure. Stir in chocolate and vinegar until blended.

Apple-Cinnamon Breakfast Risotto

Makes 6 servings

4 tablespoons (½ stick)
  butter, divided

4 medium Granny Smith
  apples (about 1½ pounds),
  peeled and diced

1½ teaspoons ground
  cinnamon, divided

1½ cups uncooked arborio rice

1 teaspoon salt

¼ teaspoon ground allspice

4 cups apple juice

2 tablespoons packed
  dark brown sugar, plus
  additional for serving

1 teaspoon vanilla

Milk, sliced almonds
  and dried cranberries
  (optional)

1 Press Sauté; melt 2 tablespoos butter in Instant Pot. Add apples and ½ teaspoon cinnamon; cook and stir about 5 minutes or until apples are softened. Transfer apples to small bowl; set aside.

2 Melt remaining 2 tablespoons butter in pot. Add rice, remaining 1 teaspoon cinnamon, salt and allspice; cook and stir 1 minute. Stir in apple juice, 2 tablespoons brown sugar and vanilla; mix well.

3 Secure lid and move pressure release valve to Sealing position. Press Pressure Cook or Manual; cook at high pressure 6 minutes.

4 When cooking is complete, press Cancel and use quick release. Press Sauté; add reserved apples to pot. Cook and stir 1 minute or until risotto reaches desired consistency. Serve with milk, almonds, cranberries and additional brown sugar, if desired.

Channa Chat (Indian-Spiced Snack Mix)

Makes 6 to 8 servings

1 cup dried chickpeas, soaked 8 hours or overnight

2 teaspoons canola oil

1 medium onion, finely chopped, divided

2 cloves garlic, minced

2 cups vegetable broth or water

1 tablespoon tomato paste

1 teaspoon salt

½ teaspoon ground cinnamon

½ teaspoon ground cumin

¼ teaspoon black pepper

1 bay leaf

½ cup balsamic vinegar

1 tablespoon packed brown sugar

1 plum tomato, chopped

½ jalapeño pepper, minced* or ¼ teaspoon ground red pepper (optional)

½ cup crisp rice cereal

3 tablespoons chopped fresh cilantro (optional)

Jalapeño peppers can sting and irritate the skin, so wear rubber gloves when handling peppers and do not touch your eyes.

1 Drain and rinse beans. Press Sauté; heat oil in Instant Pot. Add half of onion and garlic; cook and stir 2 minutes or until softened. Stir in chickpeas, broth, tomato paste, salt, cinnamon, cumin, black pepper and bay leaf; mix well.

2 Secure lid and move pressure release valve to Sealing position. Press Pressure Cook or Manual; cook at high pressure 15 minutes.

3 When cooking is complete, use natural release for 10 minutes, then release remaining pressure. Remove lid; let chickpeas cool in liquid 15 minutes.

4 Meanwhile, combine vinegar and brown sugar in small saucepan; cook over medium-low heat 5 minutes or until mixture is reduced and becomes syrupy.

5 Drain off and discard 1 cup liquid from chickpeas; remove and discard bay leaf. Toss chickpeas with tomato, remaining onion and jalapeño, if desired. Fold in rice cereal; drizzle with balsamic syrup. Garnish with cilantro.

Barley and Vegetable Risotto

Makes 4 to 6 servings

1 tablespoon olive oil

1 onion, chopped

1 cup uncooked pearled barley

2 cloves garlic, minced

1½ cups vegetable broth

8 ounces sliced mushrooms

1 large red bell pepper, diced

1 teaspoon salt

2 cups packed baby spinach

½ cup grated Parmesan cheese

¼ teaspoon black pepper

1 Press Sauté; heat oil in Instant Pot. Add onion; cook and stir 3 minutes or until softened. Add barley and garlic; cook and stir 1 minute. Stir in broth, mushrooms, bell pepper and salt; mix well.

2 Secure lid and move pressure release valve to Sealing position. Press Pressure Cook or Manual; cook at high pressure 18 minutes.

3 When cooking is complete, use natural release for 10 minutes, then release remaining pressure.

4 Stir in spinach; let stand 2 to 3 minutes or until spinach is wilted. Gently stir in cheese and black pepper.

Asian Kale and Chickpeas

Makes 4 to 6 servings

2 cups dried chickpeas, soaked 8 hours or overnight

1 tablespoon plus 1 teaspoon sesame oil, divided

1 medium onion, thinly sliced

2 teaspoons grated fresh ginger, divided

2 cloves garlic, minced, divided

2 jalapeño peppers,* finely chopped, divided

2 cups vegetable broth

½ cup water

1 teaspoon salt

8 cups loosely packed chopped kale (about 1 bunch)

1 tablespoon lime juice

1 teaspoon grated lime peel

Hot cooked rice (optional)

Jalapeño peppers can sting and irritate the skin, so wear rubber gloves when handling peppers and do not touch your eyes.

1 Drain and rinse chickpeas. Press Sauté; heat 1 tablespoon oil in Instant Pot. Add onion, 1 teaspoon ginger, 1 clove garlic and 1 jalapeño; cook and stir 3 minutes or until onion is softened. Stir in chickpeas, broth, water and salt; mix well.

2 Secure lid and move pressure release valve to Sealing position. Press Pressure Cook or Manual; cook at high pressure 15 minutes.

3 When cooking is complete, use natural release for 10 minutes, then release remaining pressure. Stir in kale. Secure lid and move pressure release valve to Sealing position. Press Pressure Cook or Manual; cook at high pressure 3 minutes.

4 When cooking is complete, press Cancel and use quick release.

5 If there is excess liquid in pot, press Sauté and cook 2 to 3 minutes or until liquid evaporates. Stir in remaining 1 teaspoon oil, 1 teaspoon ginger, 1 clove garlic, 1 jalapeño, lime juice and lime peel. Season with additional salt, if desired. Serve with rice, if desired.

Three-Bean Chili with Chorizo

Makes 6 to 8 servings

½ cup dried pinto beans, soaked 8 hours or overnight

½ cup dried kidney beans, soaked 8 hours or overnight

½ cup dried black beans, soaked 8 hours or overnight

2 uncooked Mexican chorizo sausages (about 6 ounces each), casings removed

1 tablespoon vegetable oil

1 large onion, chopped

1 tablespoon salt

1 tablespoon tomato paste

1 tablespoon minced garlic

1 tablespoon chili powder

1 tablespoon ancho chili powder

1 teaspoon chipotle chili powder

2 teaspoons ground cumin

1 teaspoon ground coriander

1 can (28 ounces) crushed tomatoes

2 cups water

Chopped fresh cilantro (optional)

1 Drain and rinse beans. Press Sauté; add chorizo to Instant Pot. Cook 3 to 4 minutes, stirring to break up meat. Remove to bowl.

2 Heat oil in pot. Add onion; cook and stir 3 minutes or until softened. Add salt, tomato paste, garlic, chili powders, cumin and coriander; cook and stir 1 minute. Stir in tomatoes, water, beans and chorizo; mix well.

3 Secure lid and move pressure release valve to Sealing position. Press Pressure Cook or Manual; cook at high pressure 20 minutes.

4 When cooking is complete, use natural release for 10 minutes, then release remaining pressure. Garnish with cilantro.

Easy Dirty Rice

Makes 4 to 6 servings

1½ cups uncooked long grain rice

8 ounces bulk Italian sausage

1½ cups water

1 onion, finely chopped

1 green bell pepper, finely chopped

½ cup finely chopped celery

1½ teaspoons salt

¼ teaspoon black pepper

¼ teaspoon ground red pepper

½ cup chopped fresh parsley

1 Rinse rice well; drain in fine-mesh strainer.

2 Press Sauté; cook sausage in Instant Pot 6 to 8 minutes or until browned, stirring to break up meat. Drain fat. Stir in rice, water, onion, bell pepper, celery, salt, black pepper and red pepper; mix well.

3 Secure lid and move pressure release valve to Sealing position. Press Pressure Cook or Manual; cook at high pressure 4 minutes.

4 When cooking is complete, use natural release for 10 minutes, then release remaining pressure. Stir in parsley.

Fruity Whole-Grain Cereal

Makes 4 to 6 servings

2¼ cups water

¼ cup steel-cut oats

¼ cup uncooked pearled
   barley

¼ cup uncooked brown rice

½ teaspoon salt

½ cup milk

⅓ cup golden raisins

¼ cup finely chopped
   dried dates

¼ cup chopped prunes

2 tablespoons packed
   brown sugar

½ teaspoon ground cinnamon

1 Combine water, oats, barley, rice and salt in Instant Pot; mix well.

2 Secure lid and move pressure release valve to Sealing position. Press Pressure Cook or Manual; cook at high pressure 20 minutes.

3 When cooking is complete, use natural release for 10 minutes, then release remaining pressure.

4 Stir in milk, raisins, dates, prunes, brown sugar and cinnamon; mix well. Serve hot.

Tip

To reheat cereal, place one serving in microwavable bowl. Microwave on HIGH 30 seconds; stir. Add water or milk to reach desired consistency; microwave just until hot.

SOUPS

Easy Corn Chowder

Makes 4 servings

6 slices bacon, chopped

1 medium onion, diced

1 red bell pepper, diced

1 stalk celery, sliced

1 package (16 ounces) frozen corn, thawed

3 small potatoes, peeled and cut into ½-inch pieces (about 2 cups)

½ teaspoon ground coriander

3 cups chicken broth

½ teaspoon salt

½ teaspoon black pepper

¼ teaspoon ground red pepper

½ cup whipping cream

1 Press Sauté; cook bacon in Instant Pot until crisp. Remove to paper towel-lined plate. Drain off all but 1 tablespoon drippings.

2 Add onion, bell pepper and celery to pot; cook and stir 3 minutes or until vegetables are softened. Add corn, potatoes and coriander; cook and stir 1 minute. Stir in broth, salt, black pepper and ground red pepper; mix well.

3 Secure lid and move pressure release valve to Sealing position. Press Pressure Cook or Manual; cook at high pressure 4 minutes.

4 When cooking is complete, use natural release for 10 minutes, then release remaining pressure.

5 Press Sauté; cook 2 to 3 minutes or until soup thickens, partially mashing potatoes. Stir in cream; cook until heated through. Top with bacon.

Turkey Vegetable Rice Soup

Makes 6 to 8 servings

- 6 cups cold water
- 2 pounds turkey drumsticks (about 3 small)
- 1 large onion, cut into 8 wedges
- 4 tablespoons soy sauce, divided
- 1 bay leaf
- ½ teaspoon salt, divided
- ½ teaspoon black pepper, divided
- 2 carrots, sliced
- 8 ounces mushrooms, sliced
- 2 cups coarsely chopped bok choy (about 6 ounces)
- ½ cup uncooked rice
- 1½ cups fresh snow peas, cut in half crosswise
- Sriracha or hot pepper sauce (optional)

1 Combine water, turkey, onion, 2 tablespoons soy sauce, bay leaf, ¼ teaspoon salt and ¼ teaspoon pepper in Instant Pot.

2 Secure lid and move pressure release valve to Sealing position. Press Pressure Cook or Manual; cook at high pressure 25 minutes.

3 When cooking is complete, use natural release for 10 minutes, then release remaining pressure. Remove turkey to plate; let stand until cool enough to handle.

4 Meanwhile, add carrots, mushrooms, bok choy, rice and remaining ¼ teaspoon salt to soup; mix well. Secure lid and move pressure release valve to Sealing position. Press Pressure Cook or Manual; cook at high pressure 4 minutes.

5 When cooking is complete, use natural release for 5 minutes, then release remaining pressure. Remove and discard bay leaf.

6 Remove turkey meat from bones; discard skin and bones. Cut turkey into bite-size pieces. Press Sauté; stir turkey, snow peas, remaining 2 tablespoons soy sauce and ¼ teaspoon pepper into soup. Cook and stir 2 to 3 minutes or until snow peas are crisp-tender. Serve with sriracha sauce, if desired.

Middle Eastern Lentil Soup

Makes 4 servings

2   tablespoons olive oil

1   small onion, chopped

1   medium red bell pepper, chopped

1   teaspoon whole fennel seeds

½   teaspoon ground cumin

¼   teaspoon ground red pepper

4   cups water

1   cup dried lentils, rinsed and sorted

1½   teaspoons salt

1   tablespoon lemon juice

½   cup plain yogurt

2   tablespoons chopped fresh parsley

1 Press Sauté; heat oil in Instant Pot. Add onion and bell pepper; cook and stir 3 minutes or until vegetables are softened. Add fennel seeds, cumin and ground red pepper; cook and stir 1 minute. Stir in water, lentils and salt; mix well.

2 Secure lid and move pressure release valve to Sealing position. Press Pressure Cook or Manual; cook at high pressure 17 minutes.

3 When cooking is complete, use natural release for 10 minutes, then release remaining pressure.

4 Stir in lemon juice. Top soup with yogurt; sprinkle with parsley.

Oxtail Soup

Makes 4 servings

2½ pounds meaty beef oxtails

1 large onion, cut in half and sliced

4 carrots, cut into ¾-inch pieces, divided

3 stalks celery, cut into ¾-inch pieces, divided

2 sprigs fresh parsley

2 cloves garlic, peeled

½ teaspoon salt

1 bay leaf

5 whole black peppercorns

2 cups beef broth

1 cup dark beer or stout

1 large russet potato, cut into 1-inch pieces

Ground black pepper

Chopped fresh parsley (optional)

1 Combine oxtails, onion, half of carrots, one third of celery, parsley sprigs, garlic, ½ teaspoon salt, bay leaf and peppercorns in Instant Pot. Stir in broth and beer.

2 Secure lid and move pressure release valve to Sealing position. Press Pressure Cook or Manual; cook at high pressure 35 minutes.

3 When cooking is complete, use natural release for 5 minutes, then release remaining pressure. Remove oxtails to plate.

4 Strain broth through large sieve or colander, pressing vegetables lightly with slotted spoon to extract all liquid. Discard vegetables. Wipe out pot with paper towels, if necessary. Return broth to pot with remaining half of carrots, two thirds of celery and potato.

5 Secure lid and move pressure release valve to Sealing position. Press Pressure Cook or Manual; cook at high pressure 3 minutes. When cooking is complete, press Cancel and use quick release.

6 Remove meat from oxtails when cool enough to handle; discard fat and bones. Press Sauté; add meat to soup. Cook 2 minutes or until heated through. Season with additional salt and pepper; garnish with chopped parsley.

Creamy Carrot Soup

Makes 4 servings

1 tablespoon butter

½ cup chopped onion

1 tablespoon chopped fresh ginger

1 pound baby carrots or regular carrots, cut into 2-inch pieces

½ teaspoon salt

¼ teaspoon black pepper

3 cups vegetable broth

¼ cup whipping cream

2 tablespoons orange juice

Pinch ground nutmeg

4 tablespoons sour cream (optional)

Fresh parsley sprigs (optional)

1 Press Sauté; melt butter in Instant Pot. Add onion and ginger; cook and stir 1 minute or until ginger is fragrant. Add carrots, salt and pepper; cook and stir 2 minutes. Stir in broth; mix well.

2 Secure lid and move pressure release valve to Sealing position. Press Pressure Cook or Manual; cook at high pressure 6 minutes.

3 When cooking is complete, use natural release for 10 minutes, then release remaining pressure.

4 Use immersion blender to blend soup until smooth. (Or purée soup in batches in food processor or blender.)

5 Press Sauté; adjust heat to low ("less"). Add cream, orange juice and nutmeg; cook until heated through, stirring frequently. (Do not boil.) Top with sour cream and parsley, if desired.

Potato Soup with Green Chiles and Cheese

Makes 4 to 6 servings

- 1 tablespoon vegetable oil
- 1 medium onion, chopped
- 1 clove garlic, minced
- 1 tablespoon all-purpose flour
- 2 cups chopped unpeeled potatoes
- 2 cups chicken broth
- ½ teaspoon salt
- ½ teaspoon celery salt, divided
- 2 cups milk
- 1 can (4 ounces) diced green chiles, drained
- ¾ cup (3 ounces) shredded Monterey Jack cheese
- ¾ cup (3 ounces) shredded Colby or Cheddar cheese

1 Press Sauté; heat oil in Instant Pot. Add onion and garlic; cook and stir 3 minutes or until softened. Stir in flour until blended. Add potatoes, broth, salt and ¼ teaspoon celery salt; mix well.

2 Secure lid and move pressure release valve to Sealing position. Press Pressure Cook or Manual; cook at high pressure 4 minutes.

3 When cooking is complete, press Cancel and use quick release.

4 Press Sauté; adjust heat to low ("less"). Add milk, chiles and remaining ¼ teaspoon celery salt; cook 5 minutes, stirring occasionally. Add Monterey Jack and Colby cheeses; cook and stir just until cheeses are melted. (Do not boil.)

Pozole

Makes 6 servings

1 tablespoon olive oil

1 large onion, halved then cut into ¼-inch slices

2 teaspoons dried oregano

1 clove garlic, minced

½ teaspoon ground cumin

12 ounces boneless skinless chicken thighs, cut into 1-inch strips

2 cans (4 ounces each) chopped green chiles

3 cups chicken broth

¼ teaspoon salt

1 package (10 ounces) frozen corn

1 can (2¼ ounces) sliced black olives, drained

Chopped fresh cilantro (optional)

Lime wedges (optional)

1 Press Sauté; heat oil in Instant Pot. Add onion; cook and stir about 3 minutes or until softened. Add oregano, garlic and cumin; cook and stir 1 minute. Stir in chicken and chiles until blended. Add broth and salt; mix well.

2 Secure lid and move pressure release valve to Sealing position. Press Pressure Cook or Manual; cook at high pressure 5 minutes.

3 When cooking is complete, use natural release for 10 minutes, then release remaining pressure.

4 Press Sauté; add corn and olives to soup. Cook and stir 3 minutes or until heated through. Garnish with cilantro; serve with lime wedges, if desired.

Tomato-Basil Soup

Makes 6 servings

- 1 tablespoon olive oil
- 1 medium onion, finely chopped
- 3 tablespoons tomato paste
- 1 tablespoon packed dark brown sugar
- 1 teaspoon salt
- ¼ teaspoon black pepper
- ¼ teaspoon ground allspice
- 1 can (28 ounces) whole tomatoes, undrained, chopped
- 2 cans (about 14 ounces each) fire-roasted diced tomatoes
- 2 cups vegetable broth
- 1 can (5 ounces) evaporated milk
- ¼ cup chopped fresh basil leaves

1 Press Sauté; heat oil in Instant Pot. Add onion; cook and stir 10 minutes or until dark brown. Add tomato paste, brown sugar, salt, pepper and allspice; cook and stir 1 minute. Stir in whole tomatoes with juice, diced tomatoes and broth; mix well.

2 Secure lid and move pressure release valve to Sealing position. Press Pressure Cook or Manual; cook at high pressure 5 minutes.

3 When cooking is complete, use natural release for 20 minutes, then release remaining pressure.

4 Press Sauté; add evaporated milk and basil to pot. Cook and stir just until heated through.

Minestrone alla Milanese

Makes 6 servings

¾ cup dried cannellini beans, soaked 8 hours or overnight

2 tablespoons olive oil

1 cup chopped carrots (½-inch pieces)

1 stalk celery, halved lengthwise and cut crosswise into ¼-inch slices

¾ cup chopped onion

2 cloves garlic, minced

1 container (32 ounces) vegetable broth

1 can (about 14 ounces) diced tomatoes

1 cup diced unpeeled red potato (about 1 large)

1 cup coarsely chopped green cabbage

1 small zucchini, halved lengthwise and cut crosswise into ¼-inch slices

¾ cup sliced fresh green beans

1½ teaspoons salt

½ teaspoon dried basil

¼ teaspoon dried rosemary

¼ teaspoon black pepper

1 bay leaf

Shredded Parmesan cheese (optional)

1 Drain and rinse dried beans. Press Sauté; heat oil in Instant Pot. Add carrots, celery and onion; cook and stir 5 minutes or until vegetables are softened. Add garlic; cook and stir 1 minute. Stir in broth, tomatoes, potato, cabbage, zucchini, green beans, salt, basil, rosemary, pepper and bay leaf; mix well.

2 Secure lid and move pressure release valve to Sealing position. Press Pressure Cook or Manual; cook at high pressure 10 minutes.

3 When cooking is complete, use natural release for 15 minutes, then release remaining pressure. Remove and discard bay leaf. Garnish with cheese.

North African Chicken Soup
Makes 4 to 6 servings

1 tablespoon vegetable oil

1 cup chopped onion

3 cloves garlic, minced

¾ teaspoon paprika

½ teaspoon ground cumin

½ teaspoon ground ginger

¼ teaspoon ground allspice

1¼ pounds peeled sweet potatoes, cut into 1-inch pieces (2½ cups)

2 cups chicken broth

1 can (about 14 ounces) whole tomatoes, undrained, cut up or crushed with hands

12 ounces boneless skinless chicken thighs, cut into 1-inch pieces

½ teaspoon salt

¼ to ½ teaspoon black pepper

Hot pepper sauce and lime juice (optional)

1 Press Sauté; heat oil in Instant Pot. Add onion; cook and stir 3 minutes or until softened. Add garlic; cook and stir 30 seconds. Add paprika, cumin, ginger and allspice; cook and stir 1 minute. Add sweet potatoes, broth, tomatoes, chicken and salt; mix well.

2 Secure lid and move pressure release valve to Sealing position. Press Pressure Cook or Manual; cook at high pressure 5 minutes.

3 When cooking is complete, use natural release for 10 minutes, then release remaining pressure. Stir in black pepper to taste. Serve with hot pepper sauce and lime juice, if desired.

Cauliflower Bisque

Makes 6 servings

- 1 head cauliflower (about 1½ pounds), broken into florets
- 1 large baking potato (about 1 pound), peeled and cut into 1-inch pieces
- 2 cans (about 14 ounces each) vegetable or chicken broth
- 1 cup chopped onion
- 1 clove garlic, minced
- 1 teaspoon salt
- ½ teaspoon dried thyme
- ⅛ teaspoon ground red pepper (optional)
- ⅛ teaspoon black pepper
- 1 can (5 ounces) evaporated milk
- 2 tablespoons butter
- 1 cup (4 ounces) shredded Cheddar cheese
- ¼ cup finely chopped fresh parsley
- ¼ cup finely chopped green onions

1 Combine cauliflower, potato, broth, onion, garlic, salt, thyme, red pepper, if desired, and black pepper in Instant Pot; mix well.

2 Secure lid and move pressure release valve to Sealing position. Press Pressure Cook or Manual; cook at high pressure 5 minutes.

3 When cooking is complete, use natural release for 10 minutes, then release remaining pressure.

4 Use immersion blender to blend soup until smooth (or purée soup in batches in food processor or blender). Stir in evaporated milk and butter until blended. Top with cheese, parsley and green onions.

Curried Parsnip Soup

Makes 6 to 8 servings

- 2 tablespoons butter or olive oil
- 1 medium yellow onion, chopped
- 2 stalks celery, diced
- 3 cloves garlic, minced
- 1 tablespoon salt
- 2 teaspoons curry powder
- ½ teaspoon grated fresh ginger
- ½ teaspoon black pepper
- 3 pounds parsnips, peeled and cut into 2-inch pieces
- 6 cups vegetable or chicken broth

  Chopped fresh chives (optional)

1 Press Sauté; melt butter in Instant Pot. Add onion and celery; cook and stir 5 minutes or until onion is translucent. Add garlic, salt, curry powder, ginger and pepper; cook and stir 1 minute. Stir in parsnips and broth; mix well.

2 Secure lid and move pressure release valve to Sealing position. Press Pressure Cook or Manual; cook at high pressure 10 minutes.

3 When cooking is complete, use natural release for 10 minutes, then release remaining pressure.

4 Use immersion blender to blend soup until smooth (or purée soup in batches in food processor or blender). Garnish with chives.

Turkey Noodle Soup

Makes 6 servings

1 tablespoon olive oil

1 onion, chopped

3 carrots, sliced

3 stalks celery, sliced

2 cloves garlic, minced

1 teaspoon poultry seasoning

2 turkey drumsticks (about 12 ounces each)

4 cups chicken broth

2 cups water

½ teaspoon salt

6 ounces uncooked egg noodles

⅓ cup chopped fresh Italian parsley

Black pepper

1 Press Sauté; heat oil in Instant Pot. Add onion; cook and stir 3 minutes or until softened. Add carrots, celery, garlic and poultry seasoning; cook and stir 3 minutes. Add drumsticks, broth, water and ½ teaspoon salt.

2 Secure lid and move pressure release valve to Sealing position. Press Pressure Cook or Manual; cook at high pressure 35 minutes.

3 When cooking is complete, use natural release for 10 minutes, then release remaining pressure. Remove turkey to plate; set aside 10 minutes or until cool enough to handle.

4 Meanwhile, press Sauté; bring soup to a boil. Add noodles to pot; cook 8 minutes or until tender, stirring occasionally.

5 Remove and discard turkey skin and bones; shred meat into bite-size pieces. Stir turkey and parsley into soup; cook until heated through. Season with additional salt and pepper.

Potato and Leek Soup

Makes 6 servings

8 ounces bacon, chopped
1 leek, chopped
1 onion, chopped
2 carrots, diced
4 cups chicken broth
3 potatoes, peeled and diced
1½ cups chopped cabbage
1½ teaspoons salt
½ teaspoon caraway seeds
½ teaspoon black pepper
1 bay leaf
½ cup sour cream
  Chopped fresh parsley
  (optional)

1 Press Sauté; cook bacon in Instant Pot until crisp. Remove to paper towel-lined plate. Drain off all but 2 tablespoons drippings.

2 Add leek, onion and carrots to pot; cook and stir about 3 minutes or until vegetables are softened. Stir in broth, scraping up browned bits from bottom of pot. Stir in potatoes, cabbage, salt, caraway seeds, pepper and bay leaf; mix well.

3 Secure lid and move pressure release valve to Sealing position. Press Pressure Cook or Manual; cook at high pressure 4 minutes.

4 When cooking is complete, use natural release for 10 minutes, then release remaining pressure. Remove and discard bay leaf.

5 Whisk ½ cup hot soup into sour cream in small bowl until blended. Add sour cream mixture and bacon to soup; mix well. Garnish with parsley.

Mushroom Barley Soup

Makes 6 to 8 servings

- 2 tablespoons olive oil
- 1 onion, chopped
- 2 carrots, chopped
- 2 stalks celery, chopped
- 3 cloves garlic, minced
- 1 teaspoon salt
- ½ teaspoon dried thyme
- ½ teaspoon black pepper
- 5 cups vegetable or chicken broth
- 1 package (16 ounces) sliced mushrooms
- ½ cup uncooked pearled barley
- ½ ounce dried porcini or shiitake mushrooms

1 Press Sauté; heat oil in Instant Pot. Add onion, carrots and celery; cook and stir 5 minutes or until vegetables are softened. Add garlic, salt, thyme and pepper; cook and stir 1 minute. Stir in broth, sliced mushrooms, barley and dried mushrooms; mix well.

2 Secure lid and move pressure release valve to Sealing position. Press Pressure Cook or Manual; cook at high pressure 22 minutes.

3 When cooking is complete, use natural release for 10 minutes, then release remaining pressure.

Spicy Squash and Chicken Soup

Makes 4 servings

1 tablespoon vegetable oil

1 small onion, finely chopped

1 stalk celery, finely chopped

2 cups chicken broth

2 cups cubed butternut squash (1-inch pieces)

1 can (about 14 ounces) diced tomatoes with chiles

8 ounces boneless skinless chicken thighs, cut into ½-inch pieces

½ teaspoon salt

½ teaspoon ground ginger

⅛ teaspoon ground cumin

⅛ teaspoon black pepper

2 teaspoons lime juice

½ to 1 teaspoon hot pepper sauce

Fresh cilantro or parsley sprigs (optional)

1 Press Sauté; heat oil in Instant Pot. Add onion and celery; cook and stir 4 minutes or until vegetables are softened. Add broth, squash, tomatoes, chicken, salt, ginger, cumin and black pepper; mix well.

2 Secure lid and move pressure release valve to Sealing position. Press Pressure Cook or Manual; cook at high pressure 5 minutes.

3 When cooking is complete, use natural release for 10 minutes, then release remaining pressure.

4 Stir in lime juice and hot pepper sauce; garnish with cilantro.

Split Pea Soup

Makes 4 to 6 servings

8 slices bacon, chopped
1 onion, chopped
2 carrots, chopped
1 stalk celery, chopped
1 clove garlic, minced
½ teaspoon dried thyme
1 container (32 ounces) chicken broth
2 cups water
1 package (16 ounces) dried split peas, rinsed and sorted
¾ teaspoon salt
½ teaspoon black pepper
1 bay leaf

1 Press Sauté; cook bacon in Instant Pot until crisp. Remove to paper towel-lined plate. Drain off all but 1 tablespoon drippings.

2 Add onion, carrots and celery to pot; cook and stir 5 minutes or until vegetables are softened. Add garlic and thyme; cook and stir 1 minute. Stir in broth and water, scraping up browned bits from bottom of pot. Add split peas, half of bacon, salt, pepper and bay leaf; mix well.

3 Secure lid and move pressure release valve to Sealing position. Press Pressure Cook or Manual; cook at high pressure 8 minutes.

4 When cooking is complete, use natural release for 10 minutes, then release remaining pressure. Stir soup; remove and discard bay leaf. Garnish with remaining bacon.

Note

The soup may seem thin immediately after cooking, but it will thicken upon standing. If prepared in advance and refrigerated, thin the soup with water when reheating until it reaches the desired consistency.

Beef and Beet Borscht

Makes 6 to 8 servings

6 slices bacon, chopped

1½ pounds boneless beef chuck roast, trimmed and cut into ½-inch pieces

1 medium onion, chopped

4 cloves garlic, minced

4 medium beets, peeled and cut into ½-inch pieces

2 large carrots, sliced

2 cups beef broth

3 tablespoons honey

3 tablespoons red wine vinegar

6 sprigs fresh dill

2 bay leaves

3 cups shredded green cabbage

1 Press Sauté; cook bacon in Instant Pot until crisp. Remove to paper towel-lined plate.

2 Add beef to pot; cook about 5 minutes or until browned. Remove to plate; drain off all but 1 tablespoon fat. Add onion to pot; cook and stir 3 minutes or until softened. Add garlic; cook and stir 30 seconds. Add beets, carrots, broth, honey, vinegar, dill and bay leaves; mix well.

3 Secure lid and move pressure release valve to Sealing position. Press Pressure Cook or Manual; cook at high pressure 25 minutes.

4 When cooking is complete, use natural release for 15 minutes, then release remaining pressure. Add cabbage to pot. Secure lid and move pressure release valve to Sealing position. Press Pressure Cook or Manual; cook at high pressure 1 minute.

5 When cooking is complete, press Cancel and use quick release. Remove and discard dill stems and bay leaves.

French Onion Soup

Makes 8 servings

¼ cup (½ stick) butter

4 medium yellow onions (about 3 pounds), sliced

1 tablespoon sugar

¾ teaspoon salt

¼ teaspoon black pepper

¼ cup dry white wine or sherry

8 cups beef broth

8 to 16 slices French bread

1 cup (4 ounces) shredded Gruyère or Swiss cheese

1 Press Sauté; melt butter in Instant Pot. Add onions; cook 15 minutes, stirring occasionally. Add sugar, salt and pepper; cook and stir 5 to 7 minutes or until onions are golden brown. Add wine; cook and stir 1 minute or until evaporated. Stir in broth; mix well.

2 Secure lid and move pressure release valve to Sealing position. Press Pressure Cook or Manual; cook at high pressure 5 minutes.

3 When cooking is complete, press Cancel and use quick release. Preheat broiler.

4 Ladle soup into individual ovenproof bowls; top with 1 or 2 slices bread and about 2 tablespoons cheese. Place bowls on large baking sheet. Broil 1 to 2 minutes or until bread is toasted and cheese is melted and browned.

POULTRY

Pesto Turkey Meatballs

Makes 4 servings

1 pound ground turkey

⅓ cup prepared pesto

⅓ cup grated Parmesan cheese, plus additional for garnish

¼ cup panko bread crumbs

1 egg

2 green onions, finely chopped

½ teaspoon salt, divided

2 tablespoons olive oil

2 cloves garlic, minced

⅛ teaspoon red pepper flakes

1 can (28 ounces) whole tomatoes, undrained, crushed with hands or coarsely chopped

1 tablespoon tomato paste

Hot cooked pasta (optional)

Chopped fresh basil (optional)

1 Combine turkey, pesto, ⅓ cup cheese, panko, egg, green onions and ¼ teaspoon salt in medium bowl; mix well. Shape mixture into 24 balls (about 1¼ inches). Refrigerate meatballs while preparing sauce.

2 Press Sauté; heat oil in Instant Pot. Add garlic and red pepper flakes; cook and stir 1 minute. Add tomatoes with liquid, tomato paste and remaining ¼ teaspoon salt; cook 3 minutes or until sauce begins to simmer, stirring occasionally.

3 Remove about 1 cup sauce from pot. Arrange meatballs in single layer in pot; pour reserved sauce over meatballs.

4 Secure lid and move pressure release valve to Sealing position. Press Pressure Cook or Manual; cook at high pressure 10 minutes.

5 When cooking is complete, use natural release for 10 minutes, then release remaining pressure. If sauce is too thin, press Sauté and cook 5 minutes or until sauce thickens, stirring frequently. Serve over pasta; garnish with additional cheese and basil, if desired.

Tuscan Chicken Breasts

Makes 6 servings

Polenta (recipe follows, optional)

6 plum tomatoes, coarsely chopped

½ teaspoon salt, divided

½ teaspoon garlic powder

½ teaspoon Italian seasoning

¾ teaspoon black pepper, divided

6 boneless skinless chicken breasts (about 8 ounces each)

1 tablespoon vegetable oil

½ cup chopped onion

2 cloves garlic, minced

1 can (8 ounces) tomato sauce

2 teaspoons dried basil

2 teaspoons dried oregano

2 teaspoons dried rosemary

1 Prepare and refrigerate Polenta up to a day in advance, if desired.

2 Place tomatoes in colander; toss with ¼ teaspoon salt. Let tomatoes drain while preparing chicken. Combine garlic powder, Italian seasoning, remaining ¼ teaspoon salt and ¼ teaspoon pepper in small bowl; mix well. Rub spice mixture into both sides of chicken.

3 Press Sauté; heat oil in Instant Pot. Add chicken in batches; cook about 8 minutes or until browned on both sides. Remove chicken to plate.

4 Add onion to pot; cook and stir 3 minutes or until beginning to brown. Add garlic; cook and stir 15 seconds. Stir in drained plum tomatoes, tomato sauce, basil, oregano, rosemary and remaining ½ teaspoon pepper, scraping up browned bits from bottom of pot. Return chicken to pot, pressing into tomato mixture.

5 Secure lid and move pressure release valve to Sealing position. Press Pressure Cook or Manual; cook at high pressure 6 minutes.

6 When cooking is complete, press Cancel and use quick release. Remove chicken to clean plate; tent with foil. Press Sauté; cook sauce about 10 minutes or until slightly thickened, stirring occasionally. Serve sauce with chicken and polenta, if desired.

Polenta

Bring 4 cups chicken broth to a boil in large saucepan over high heat. Slowly stir in 1 cup polenta (not instant) or yellow cornmeal. Reduce heat to low; cook 15 to 20 minutes or until very thick, stirring frequently. (Mixture may be lumpy.) Pour polenta into greased 9×5-inch loaf pan. Cool to room temperature; cover and refrigerate 2 to 3 hours or until firm. To serve, remove from pan and cut crosswise into 16 slices. Cut slices into triangles, if desired. Spray large nonstick skillet with nonstick cooking spray; cook polenta over medium heat about 4 minutes per side or until lightly browned.

Quick Chicken and Bean Stew

Makes 4 to 6 servings

1 pound boneless skinless chicken thighs, cut into 1-inch pieces

1 can (about 15 ounces) Great Northern beans, rinsed and drained

1 can (about 15 ounces) black beans, rinsed and drained

1 can (about 14 ounces) crushed tomatoes (preferably fire-roasted)

1 onion, chopped

⅓ cup chicken broth

Juice of 1 large orange (about ⅓ cup)

1 canned chipotle pepper in adobo sauce, minced

1 teaspoon salt

1 teaspoon ground cumin

1 bay leaf

Fresh cilantro sprigs (optional)

1 Combine chicken, beans, tomatoes, onion, broth, orange juice, chipotle pepper, salt, cumin and bay leaf in Instant Pot; mix well.

2 Secure lid and move pressure release valve to Sealing position. Press Pressure Cook or Manual; cook at high pressure 6 minutes.

3 When cooking is complete, use natural release for 5 minutes, then release remaining pressure.

4 Press Sauté; cook 3 to 5 minutes or until stew thickens, stirring frequently. Remove and discard bay leaf. Garnish with cilantro.

Provençal Lemon and Olive Chicken

Makes 4 servings

2 cups chopped onions

2½ pounds bone-in skinless chicken thighs (about 6)

1 lemon, thinly sliced and seeded

1 cup pitted green olives

1 tablespoon olive brine or white vinegar

2 teaspoons herbes de Provence*

1 bay leaf

1 teaspoon salt

¼ teaspoon black pepper

⅓ cup chicken broth

½ cup minced fresh Italian parsley

Hot cooked rice (optional)

Or substitute ½ teaspoon each dried rosemary, thyme, sage and savory.

1 Place onions in Instant Pot. Arrange chicken over onions; top with lemon slices. Add olives, brine, herbes de Provence, bay leaf, salt and pepper. Pour in broth.

2 Secure lid and move pressure release valve to Sealing position. Press Pressure Cook or Manual; cook at high pressure 10 minutes.

3 When cooking is complete, press Cancel and use quick release. Remove chicken to plate; tent with foil.

4 Press Sauté; cook about 5 minutes or until sauce is reduced by one third. Remove and discard bay leaf; stir in parsley. Serve sauce with chicken and rice, if desired.

Chili Turkey Breast with Cilantro-Lime Rice

Makes 6 to 8 servings

Turkey

- 1½ tablespoons chili powder
- 2 teaspoons dried oregano
- 1½ teaspoons ground cumin
- ½ teaspoon red pepper flakes
- ½ teaspoon salt
- ½ teaspoon black pepper
- 1 boneless turkey breast (about 4 pounds), skin removed
- 1 cup chicken broth

Rice

- 1½ cups uncooked long grain rice
- ¾ cup water
- 2 medium red bell peppers, chopped
- 1 cup chopped green onions
- ½ cup chopped fresh cilantro
- 2 tablespoons lime juice
- 1 tablespoon grated lime peel
- 1 tablespoon olive oil
- ½ teaspoon ground turmeric (optional)
- ¼ teaspoon salt

1 Combine chili powder, oregano, cumin, red pepper flakes, ½ teaspoon salt and black pepper in small bowl; mix well. Rub into all sides of turkey. Pour broth into Instant Pot. Place rack in pot; place turkey on rack.

2 Secure lid and move pressure release valve to Sealing position. Press Pressure Cook or Manual; cook at high pressure 35 minutes.

3 When cooking is complete, use natural release for 10 minutes, then release remaining pressure. Remove turkey to cutting board; tent with foil. Reserve ¾ cup cooking liquid for rice; discard remaining liquid. Wipe out pot with paper towels.

4 Rinse rice well; drain in fine-mesh strainer. Combine rice, reserved ¾ cup cooking liquid, water, bell peppers, green onions, cilantro, lime juice, lime peel, oil, turmeric, if desired, and ¼ teaspoon salt in pot; mix well.

5 Secure lid and move pressure release valve to Sealing position. Press Pressure Cook or Manual; cook at high pressure 4 minutes.

6 When cooking is complete, use natural release for 10 minutes, then release remaining pressure. Fluff rice gently with fork. Slice turkey; serve with rice.

Indian-Style Apricot Chicken

Makes 4 to 6 servings

2½ pounds bone-in skinless chicken thighs (about 6)

½ teaspoon salt

¼ teaspoon black pepper

1 tablespoon vegetable oil

1 large onion, chopped

½ cup chicken broth, divided

1 tablespoon grated fresh ginger

2 cloves garlic, minced

½ teaspoon ground cinnamon

⅛ teaspoon ground allspice

1 can (about 14 ounces) diced tomatoes

1 package (8 ounces) dried apricots

Pinch saffron threads (optional)

Hot cooked basmati rice (optional)

Chopped fresh Italian parsley (optional)

1 Season both sides of chicken with ½ teaspoon salt and ¼ teaspoon pepper. Press Sauté; heat oil in Instant Pot. Add chicken in batches; cook about 8 minutes or until browned on both sides. Remove to plate.

2 Add onion and 2 tablespoons broth to pot; cook and stir 5 minutes or until onion is translucent, scraping up browned bits from bottom of pot. Add ginger, garlic, cinnamon and allspice; cook and stir 30 seconds or until fragrant. Stir in tomatoes, apricots, remaining broth and saffron, if desired; mix well. Return chicken to pot, pressing into liquid.

3 Secure lid and move pressure release valve to Sealing position. Press Pressure Cook or Manual; cook at high pressure 11 minutes.

4 When cooking is complete, press Cancel and use quick release. Season with additional salt and pepper. Serve with rice, if desired. Garnish with parsley.

Tip

To remove chicken skin easily, use paper towel to grasp skin and pull away.

Italian Country-Style Chicken

Makes 4 servings

½ cup dried porcini mushrooms (about ½ ounce)

1 cup boiling water

⅓ cup all-purpose flour

1 teaspoon salt

½ teaspoon black pepper

1 cut-up whole chicken (3½ to 4 pounds)*

2 tablespoons olive oil

1 medium onion, chopped

2 carrots, cut diagonally into ¼-inch slices

3 ounces pancetta,* chopped (about ½ cup)

3 cloves garlic, minced

1 tablespoon tomato paste

1 cup pitted green Italian olives

Or use 2 leg quarters and 2 breasts and cut each into two pieces.

**Or substitute 3 ounces bacon.*

1 Place mushrooms in small bowl; pour boiling water over mushrooms. Let stand 15 to 20 minutes or until mushrooms are softened.

2 Meanwhile, combine flour, 1 teaspoon salt and ½ teaspoon pepper in large resealable food storage bag. Add 1 or 2 pieces of chicken at a time; toss to coat.

3 Press Sauté; heat oil in Instant Pot. Add chicken in two batches; cook until browned on both sides. Remove to plate. Pour off all but 1 tablespoon fat.

4 Drain mushrooms; reserve and strain soaking liquid. Chop mushrooms. Add onion, carrots and pancetta to pot; cook and stir 5 minutes. Add garlic and tomato paste; cook and stir 1 minute. Add reserved mushroom liquid; cook 2 minutes, scraping up browned bits from bottom of pot. Stir in mushrooms; mix well. Return chicken to pot, pressing into liquid.

5 Secure lid and move pressure release valve to Sealing position. Press Pressure Cook or Manual; cook at high pressure 10 minutes.

6 When cooking is complete, press Cancel and use quick release. Remove chicken to platter; tent with foil.

7 Press Sauté. Add olives; cook about 2 minutes or until heated through and sauce thickens slightly, stirring frequently. Season with additional salt and pepper, if desired. Pour sauce over chicken.

Hearty Chicken Chili

Makes 4 servings

- 1 tablespoon vegetable oil
- 1 onion, finely chopped
- 1 jalapeño pepper,* minced
- 1 clove garlic, minced
- 1½ teaspoons chili powder
- ¾ teaspoon salt
- ½ teaspoon ground cumin
- ½ teaspoon dried oregano
- ½ teaspoon black pepper
- ¼ teaspoon red pepper flakes (optional)
- 1 cup chicken broth
- 1½ pounds boneless skinless chicken thighs, cut into 1-inch pieces
- 2 cans (about 15 ounces each) hominy, rinsed and drained
- 1 can (about 15 ounces) pinto beans, rinsed and drained
- 1 tablespoon all-purpose flour (optional)

  Chopped fresh cilantro (optional)

Jalapeño peppers can sting and irritate the skin, so wear rubber gloves when handling peppers and do not touch your eyes.

1 Press Sauté; heat oil in Instant Pot. Add onion; cook and stir 3 minutes or until softened. Add jalapeño, garlic, chili powder, salt, cumin, oregano, black pepper and red pepper flakes, if desired; cook and stir 30 seconds. Stir in broth; cook 1 minute. Add chicken, hominy and beans; mix well.

2 Secure lid and move pressure release valve to Sealing position. Press Pressure Cook or Manual; cook at high pressure 6 minutes.

3 When cooking is complete, use natural release for 10 minutes, then release remaining pressure.

4 For thicker chili, stir 1 tablespoon flour into 3 tablespoons cooking liquid in small bowl until smooth. Press Sauté; add flour mixture to chili. Cook about 5 minutes or until chili thickens, stirring occasionally. Garnish with cilantro.

Barbecue Turkey Drumsticks

Makes 4 servings

⅓ cup white vinegar

⅓ cup ketchup

⅓ cup molasses

2 tablespoons Worcestershire sauce

2 teaspoons onion powder

2 teaspoons garlic powder

¾ teaspoon liquid smoke

⅛ teaspoon chipotle chili powder

4 turkey drumsticks (8 to 12 ounces each)

1¼ teaspoons salt

1¼ teaspoons black pepper

1 Combine vinegar, ketchup, molasses, Worcestershire sauce, onion powder, garlic powder, liquid smoke and chipotle chili powder in measuring cup or medium bowl; mix well.

2 Season drumsticks with salt and pepper; place in Instant Pot. Pour sauce over drumsticks, turning to coat completely.

3 Secure lid and move pressure release valve to Sealing position. Press Pressure Cook or Manual; cook at high pressure 35 minutes.

4 When cooking is complete, use natural release. Remove drumsticks from pot; let stand 10 minutes before serving. Serve with remaining sauce.

Chicken Congee

Makes 6 servings

4 cups water

4 cups chicken broth

2 chicken leg quarters *or* 4 chicken drumsticks, skin removed (1 to 1½ pounds)

1 cup uncooked white jasmine rice, rinsed well and drained

1 (1-inch) piece fresh ginger, cut into ¼-inch slices

1 teaspoon salt

½ teaspoon white pepper

Optional toppings: soy sauce, sesame oil, sliced green onions, shredded carrot, salted roasted peanuts and/or pickled vegetables

1 Combine water, broth, chicken, rice, ginger, salt and pepper in Instant Pot; mix well.

2 Secure lid and move pressure release valve to Sealing position. Press Pressure Cook or Manual; cook at high pressure 20 minutes.

3 When cooking is complete, use natural release for 15 minutes, then release remaining pressure. Remove and discard ginger. Remove chicken to plate; set aside until cool enough to handle.

4 Meanwhile, press Sauté; cook and stir congee 2 to 3 minutes or until desired consistency is reached. Shred chicken; stir into congee. Serve with desired toppings.

Basque Chicken with Peppers

Makes 4 servings

1 cut-up whole chicken
  (3½ to 4 pounds)*

2 teaspoons salt, divided

1 teaspoon black pepper,
  divided

1½ tablespoons olive oil

1 onion, chopped

2 red, yellow or green
  bell peppers (or a
  combination), cut into
  strips

8 ounces small brown
  mushrooms, halved

2 cloves garlic, minced

1 teaspoon smoked paprika

½ teaspoon dried thyme

1 can (about 14 ounces)
  stewed tomatoes

2 tablespoons tomato paste

1 tablespoon all-purpose
  flour (optional)

2 tablespoons water
  (optional)

4 ounces chopped prosciutto

*Or use 2 leg quarters and
2 breasts and cut each into
two pieces.*

1 Season chicken with 1 teaspoon salt and
½ teaspoon black pepper. Press Sauté; heat
oil in Instant Pot. Add chicken in batches;
cook about 8 minutes or until browned on
all sides. Remove to plate.

2 Add onion to pot; cook and stir 3 minutes
or until softened. Add bell peppers and
mushrooms; cook and stir 4 minutes or until
mushrooms have released their liquid. Add
garlic, smoked paprika and thyme; cook and
stir 1 minute. Stir in tomatoes, tomato paste,
remaining 1 teaspoon salt and ½ teaspoon
black pepper; mix well. Return chicken to
pot, arranging legs and thighs on bottom
and breasts on top. Spoon some of tomato
mixture over chicken.

3 Secure lid and move pressure release valve
to Sealing position. Press Pressure Cook or
Manual; cook at high pressure 10 minutes.

4 When cooking is complete, press Cancel
and use quick release. Remove chicken
to clean plate; tent with foil.

5 If thicker sauce is desired, stir flour into
water in small bowl until smooth. Press
Sauté; add flour mixture to pot and cook
about 5 minutes or until sauce is thickened,
stirring frequently. Serve sauce with chicken;
sprinkle with prosciutto.

Cuban-Style Curried Turkey

Makes 4 servings

- 2 tablespoons all-purpose flour
- 1 teaspoon salt
- ¼ teaspoon black pepper
- 1 pound boneless turkey breast meat or turkey tenderloins, cut into 1-inch pieces
- 2 tablespoons vegetable oil, divided
- 1 onion, chopped
- ½ cup chicken broth, divided
- 1 clove garlic, minced
- ½ teaspoon curry powder
- ⅛ teaspoon red pepper flakes
- 1 can (about 15 ounces) black beans, rinsed and drained
- 1 can (about 14 ounces) diced tomatoes
- ⅓ cup raisins
- Juice of ½ lime (1 tablespoon)
- 1 tablespoon minced fresh cilantro (optional)
- 1 tablespoon minced green onion (optional)
- Hot cooked rice (optional)

1 Combine flour, salt and black pepper in large resealable food storage bag. Add turkey; shake to coat. Press Sauté; heat 1 tablespoon oil in Instant Pot. Add turkey: cook about 5 minutes or until browned, stirring occasionally. Remove to plate.

2 Add remaining 1 tablespoon oil, onion and ¼ cup broth to pot; cook and stir 3 minutes, scraping up browned bits from bottom of pot. Add garlic, curry powder and red pepper flakes; cook and stir 30 seconds. Stir in beans, tomatoes, raisins and remaining ¼ cup broth; mix well.

3 Secure lid and move pressure release valve to Sealing position. Press Pressure Cook or Manual; cook at high pressure 5 minutes.

4 When cooking is complete, press Cancel and use quick release.

5 Press Sauté; cook 3 minutes or until sauce is reduced and thickens slightly. Stir in lime juice; garnish with cilantro and green onion. Serve over rice, if desired.

Coq au Vin

Makes 4 to 6 servings

4 slices thick-cut bacon, cut into ½-inch pieces

8 bone-in skinless chicken thighs (3½ to 4 pounds)

1 teaspoon salt

½ teaspoon black pepper

1 package (8 to 10 ounces) cremini or white mushrooms, quartered

3 medium carrots, cut into 1½-inch pieces

1 tablespoon tomato paste

2 cloves garlic, minced

10 sprigs fresh thyme

1½ cups dry red wine

8 ounces frozen pearl onions (about 1½ cups), divided

1 bay leaf

1 tablespoon butter, softened

1 tablespoon all-purpose flour

Chopped fresh parsley (optional)

1 Press Sauté; cook bacon in Instant Pot until crisp. Remove to paper towel-lined plate.

2 Season both sides of chicken with 1 teaspoon salt and ½ teaspoon pepper. Add chicken to drippings in pot in two batches; cook about 8 minutes per side or until browned on both sides. Remove to plate.

3 Add mushrooms and carrots to pot; cook about 6 minutes or until mushrooms have released their liquid and begin to brown, stirring occasionally and scraping up browned bits from bottom of pot. Add tomato paste, garlic and thyme; cook and stir 2 minutes. Stir in wine; cook about 10 minutes or until reduced by half. Return chicken to pot with half of onions, half of bacon and bay leaf.

4 Secure lid and move pressure release valve to Sealing position. Press Pressure Cook or Manual; cook at high pressure 14 minutes. Meanwhile, mix butter and flour in small bowl until well blended.

5 When cooking is complete, press Cancel and use quick release. Remove chicken and vegetables to platter with slotted spoon. Remove and discard thyme sprigs and bay leaf. Press Sauté; add remaining half of onions and butter mixture to pot. Cook and stir 2 to 3 minutes or until sauce thickens. Season with additional salt and pepper, if desired. Pour sauce over chicken and vegetables. Garnish with reserved bacon and parsley, if desired.

Butter Chicken

Makes 4 to 6 servings

2 tablespoons butter

1 onion, chopped

4 cloves garlic, minced

1 teaspoon minced fresh ginger

1 teaspoon ground turmeric

1 teaspoon ground coriander

1 teaspoon garam masala

1 teaspoon ground cumin

½ teaspoon ground red pepper

½ teaspoon paprika

1 can (14 ounces) diced tomatoes

¾ teaspoon salt

2 pounds boneless skinless chicken breasts, cut into 2-inch pieces

½ cup whipping cream

Chopped fresh cilantro

Hot cooked rice (optional)

1 Press Sauté; melt butter in Instant Pot. Add onion; cook and stir about 4 minutes or until onion begins to turn golden. Add garlic and ginger; cook and stir 1 minute. Add turmeric, coriander, garam masala, cumin, red pepper and paprika; cook and stir 30 seconds. Add tomatoes and salt; cook and stir 2 minutes. Stir in chicken; mix well.

2 Secure lid and move pressure release valve to Sealing position. Press Pressure Cook or Manual; cook at high pressure 8 minutes.

3 When cooking is complete, use natural release for 10 minutes, then release remaining pressure.

4 Press Sauté; adjust heat to low ("less"). Stir in cream; cook 5 minutes or until heated through. Sprinkle with cilantro; serve with rice, if desired.

Mustard, Garlic and Herb Turkey Breast

Makes 4 to 6 servings

1 tablespoon vegetable oil

1 boneless turkey breast (about 3½ pounds), skin removed

2 tablespoons spicy brown mustard

2 tablespoons chopped fresh parsley

1 tablespoon chopped fresh thyme *or* 1 teaspoon dried thyme

1 tablespoon chopped fresh sage *or* 1 teaspoon dried sage

1 clove garlic, minced

1 teaspoon salt

½ teaspoon black pepper

1½ cups water

¼ cup all-purpose flour (optional)

1 Press Sauté; heat oil in Instant Pot. Add turkey; cook about 10 minutes or until browned on all sides.

2 Meanwhile, combine mustard, parsley, thyme, sage, garlic, salt and pepper in small bowl; mix well. Remove turkey from pot; rub herb mixture over turkey. Pour water into pot. Place rack in pot; place turkey on rack.

3 Secure lid and move pressure release valve to Sealing position. Press Pressure Cook or Manual; cook at high pressure 30 minutes.

4 When cooking is complete, use natural release for 10 minutes, then release remaining pressure. Remove turkey to cutting board; tent with foil. Let stand 10 minutes before slicing.

5 If desired, prepare gravy with cooking liquid. Stir ½ cup cooking liquid into flour in small bowl until smooth. Press Sauté; add flour mixture to pot. Cook 5 minutes or until gravy thickens, stirring frequently.

Braised Chicken with Vegetables

Makes 2 to 4 servings

- ¾ cup chicken broth
- 2 tablespoons lemon juice
- 2 cloves garlic, minced
- 1½ teaspoons Italian seasoning
- ¾ teaspoon cornstarch
- ½ teaspoon salt
- ½ teaspoon dried rosemary
- ½ teaspoon paprika
- ¼ teaspoon black pepper
- 4 chicken drumsticks, skin removed
- 1 yellow squash, cut into ½-inch pieces
- 1 zucchini, cut into ½-inch pieces
- 1 onion, cut into ½-inch pieces
- 1 small red bell pepper, cut into ½-inch pieces

1 Combine broth, lemon juice, garlic, Italian seasoning, cornstarch, salt, rosemary, paprika and black pepper in Instant Pot; mix well. Add chicken; stir to coat.

2 Secure lid and move pressure release valve to Sealing position. Press Pressure Cook or Manual; cook at high pressure 10 minutes.

3 When cooking is complete, press Cancel and use quick release.

4 Add squash, zucchini, onion and bell pepper to pot; press into cooking liquid. Press Manual; cook at high pressure 1 minute. When cooking is complete, press Cancel and use quick release. Remove chicken and vegetables to platter with slotted spoon; tent with foil.

5 Press Sauté; cook about 5 minutes or until sauce is slightly reduced. Serve sauce over chicken and vegetables.

Hoisin Barbecue Chicken Sliders

Makes 16 sliders

⅔ cup hoisin sauce

⅓ cup barbecue sauce

1 tablespoon soy sauce

¼ teaspoon red pepper flakes

3 to 3½ pounds boneless, skinless chicken thighs

2 tablespoons water

1 tablespoon cornstarch

16 dinner rolls or Hawaiian sweet rolls, split

½ medium red onion, finely chopped

Sliced pickles (optional)

1 Combine hoisin sauce, barbecue sauce, soy sauce and red pepper flakes in Instant Pot; mix well. Add chicken; stir to coat.

2 Secure lid and move pressure release valve to Sealing position. Press Pressure Cook or Manual; cook at high pressure 8 minutes.

3 When cooking is complete, use natural release for 5 minutes, then release remaining pressure. Remove chicken to plate; let stand until cool enough to handle. Shred chicken into bite-size pieces.

4 Stir water into cornstarch in small bowl until smooth. Press Sauté; add cornstarch mixture to pot. Cook and stir about 2 minutes or until sauce thickens. Return chicken to pot; mix well. Spoon about ¼ cup chicken onto each roll; serve with onion and pickles, if desired.

Chicken Enchilada Chili

Makes 4 servings

1 can (about 14 ounces) diced tomatoes with green chiles

1 can (10 ounces) red enchilada sauce

½ teaspoon salt

¼ teaspoon ground cumin

⅛ teaspoon black pepper

1½ pounds boneless skinless chicken thighs, cut into 1-inch pieces

1 cup frozen or canned corn

1½ tablespoons cornmeal

2 tablespoons finely chopped fresh cilantro

½ cup (2 ounces) shredded pepper jack cheese

Sliced green onions

1 Combine tomatoes, enchilada sauce, salt, cumin and pepper in Instant Pot; mix well. Add chicken; stir to coat.

2 Secure lid and move pressure release valve to Sealing position. Press Pressure Cook or Manual; cook at high pressure 5 minutes.

3 When cooking is complete, use natural release for 10 minutes, then release remaining pressure.

4 Press Sauté; add corn and cornmeal to pot. Cook about 6 minutes or until chili thickens, stirring frequently. Stir in cilantro. Sprinkle with cheese and green onions.

Spicy Peanut Turkey

Makes 4 to 6 servings

1½ pounds turkey tenderloins, cut into ¾-inch pieces

½ cup plus 2 tablespoons chicken broth, divided

2 tablespoons soy sauce

3 cloves garlic, minced

½ teaspoon red pepper flakes

¼ teaspoon salt

1 red bell pepper, cut into short, thin strips

3 green onions, cut into ½-inch pieces

⅓ cup creamy or chunky peanut butter (not natural-style)

1 tablespoon cornstarch

⅓ cup roasted peanuts, chopped

⅓ cup chopped fresh cilantro

Hot cooked rice noodles or egg noodles (optional)

1 Combine turkey, ½ cup broth, soy sauce, garlic, red pepper flakes and salt in Instant Pot; mix well.

2 Secure lid and move pressure release valve to Sealing position. Press Pressure Cook or Manual; cook at high pressure 5 minutes.

3 When cooking is complete, press Cancel and use quick release.

4 Press Sauté; add bell pepper, green onions and peanut butter to pot. Cook 3 minutes or until bell pepper is crisp-tender, stirring frequently.

5 Stir remaining 2 tablespoons broth into cornstarch in small bowl until smooth. Add cornstarch mixture to pot; cook 2 minutes or until sauce thickens, stirring constantly. Sprinkle with peanuts and cilantro; serve over noodles, if desired.

MEAT

Pressure Cooker Meat Loaf

Makes 6 servings

1 tablespoon olive oil

1 small onion, finely chopped

½ red bell pepper, finely chopped

3 cloves garlic, minced

1 teaspoon dried oregano

1½ cups water

2 pounds ground meat loaf mix or 1 pound *each* ground beef and ground pork

1 egg

3 tablespoons tomato paste

1 teaspoon salt

½ teaspoon black pepper

1 Press Sauté; heat oil in Instant Pot. Add onion, bell pepper, garlic and oregano; cook and stir 3 minutes or until vegetables are softened. Remove to large bowl; let cool 5 minutes. Wipe out pot with paper towels; add water and rack to pot.

2 Add meat loaf mix, egg, tomato paste, salt and black pepper to vegetable mixture; mix well. Tear off 18×12-inch piece of foil; fold in half crosswise to create 12×9-inch rectangle. Shape meat mixture into 7×5-inch oval on foil; bring up sides of foil to create pan, leaving top of meat loaf uncovered. Place foil with meat loaf on rack in pot.

3 Secure lid and move pressure release valve to Sealing position. Press Pressure Cook or Manual; cook at high pressure 37 minutes.

4 When cooking is complete, press Cancel and use quick release. Remove meat loaf to cutting board; tent with foil. Let stand 10 minutes before slicing.

Greek Beef Stew

Makes 4 to 6 servings

¼ cup all-purpose flour

2 teaspoons Greek seasoning

¼ teaspoon salt

¼ teaspoon black pepper

2 pounds bottom round or boneless beef chuck roast, cut into 1-inch pieces

2 tablespoons olive oil

½ cup beef broth

¼ cup tomato paste

1 pint grape or cherry tomatoes, divided

2 medium onions, each cut into 8 wedges

1 cup pitted kalamata olives

4 sprigs fresh oregano, plus additional for garnish

1 lemon, divided

1 Combine flour, Greek seasoning, salt and pepper in large resealable food storage bag. Add beef; shake to coat.

2 Press Sauté; heat oil in Instant Pot. Cook beef in two batches about 5 minutes or until browned. Remove to plate. Add broth and tomato paste to pot; cook and stir 2 minutes, scraping up browned bits from bottom of pot. Stir in beef, ½ cup grape tomatoes, onions, olives, 4 sprigs oregano and juice of ½ lemon; mix well.

3 Secure lid and move pressure release valve to Sealing position. Press Pressure Cook or Manual; cook at high pressure 20 minutes.

4 When cooking is complete, use natural release for 10 minutes, then release remaining pressure.

5 Press Sauté; add remaining grape tomatoes to pot. Cook about 5 minutes or until tomatoes have softened and stew thickens, stirring frequently. Cut remaining ½ lemon into wedges; serve with stew. Garnish with additional oregano.

Pork Loin with Apples and Onions

Makes 4 servings

2 tablespoons vegetable oil

1 bone-in or boneless
   pork loin roast (about
   3 pounds), trimmed

2 medium onions, chopped

2 sweet-tart apples such as
   Braeburn, Honeycrisp
   or Jonagold, peeled
   and thinly sliced

¾ cup lager beer

2 tablespoons packed
   brown sugar

1 teaspoon ground ginger

½ teaspoon salt

½ teaspoon ground cinnamon

½ teaspoon black pepper

⅛ teaspoon ground red
   pepper

1 Press Sauté; heat oil in Instant Pot. Add pork; cook about 8 minutes or until browned on all sides. Remove to plate.

2 Add onions to pot; cook and stir 5 minutes or until lightly browned. Add apples, beer, brown sugar, ginger, salt, cinnamon, black pepper and red pepper; cook and stir 1 minute, scraping up browned bits from bottom of pot. Return pork to pot.

3 Secure lid and move pressure release valve to Sealing position. Press Pressure Cook or Manual; cook at high pressure 35 minutes.

4 When cooking is complete, use natural release for 10 minutes, then release remaining pressure. Remove pork to cutting board; tent with foil.

5 Press Sauté; cook about 10 minutes or until sauce is reduced by one third, stirring occasionally. Serve with pork.

Tip

Pork should be cooked to an internal temperature of at least 145°F. Use an instant-read thermometer to check the temperature of the pork after releasing the pressure. If necessary, cook an additional few minutes.

Saucy BBQ Short Ribs

Makes 4 servings

¾ cup regular cola (not diet)

1 can (6 ounces) tomato paste

⅓ cup plus 1 tablespoon honey, divided

⅓ cup cider vinegar

2 cloves garlic, minced

1 teaspoon salt

1 teaspoon black pepper

Dash hot pepper sauce (optional)

4 pounds bone-in beef short ribs, trimmed and cut into 2-inch pieces

1 Combine cola, tomato paste, ⅓ cup honey, vinegar, garlic, salt, black pepper and hot pepper sauce, if desired, in Instant Pot; mix well. Add short ribs; turn to coat with sauce.

2 Secure lid and move pressure release valve to Sealing position. Press Pressure Cook or Manual; cook at high pressure 30 minutes.

3 When cooking is complete, use natural release for 10 minutes, then release remaining pressure. Remove short ribs to plate; tent with foil.

4 Skim excess fat from surface of sauce. Press Sauté; cook 10 to 15 minutes or until sauce is reduced by one third. Add remaining 1 tablespoon honey; cook and stir 1 minute. Brush short ribs with sauce; serve remaining sauce on the side.

Tip

For a thicker sauce, whisk 2 tablespoons water into 2 tablespoons cornstarch in a small bowl until smooth. Add to the sauce with the honey in step 4; cook and stir 1 minute or until sauce thickens.

One-Pot Pasta with Sausage

Makes 6 servings

1 tablespoon olive oil

1 pound smoked sausage (about 4 links), cut into ¼-inch pieces

1 onion, diced

1 tablespoon tomato paste

2 cloves garlic, minced

1½ teaspoons dried oregano

¼ teaspoon red pepper flakes

1 can (28 ounces) whole tomatoes, undrained, crushed with hands or coarsely chopped

2½ cups water

1½ teaspoons salt

1 package (16 ounces) uncooked cellentani pasta

1½ cups frozen peas

½ cup grated Parmesan cheese

⅓ cup chopped fresh basil leaves, plus additional for garnish

1 Press Sauté; heat oil in Instant Pot. Add sausage; cook about 7 minutes or until browned, stirring occasionally. Add onion; cook and stir 3 minutes or until softened. Add tomato paste, garlic, oregano and red pepper flakes; cook and stir 1 minute. Add tomatoes with liquid, water and salt; cook 2 minutes, scraping up browned bits from bottom of pot. Stir in pasta; mix well.

2 Secure lid and move pressure release valve to Sealing position. Press Pressure Cook or Manual; cook at high pressure 5 minutes.

3 When cooking is complete, use natural release for 5 minutes, then release remaining pressure.

4 Press Sauté; add peas to pot. Cook and stir 2 minutes. Turn off heat; stir in cheese and ⅓ cup basil. Cover pot with lid (do not lock) and let stand 2 minutes. Garnish with additional basil.

Variation

You can substitute 1 pound uncooked Italian sausage (about 4 links) for the smoked sausage. Remove the casings, cut into ½-inch pieces and proceed with the recipe as directed.

Jerk Pork and Sweet Potato Stew

Makes 4 servings

2 tablespoons all-purpose flour

1 teaspoon salt

¼ teaspoon black pepper

1¼ pounds boneless pork shoulder, cut into 1-inch pieces

2 tablespoons vegetable oil

4 tablespoons minced green onions, divided

1 small jalapeño pepper,* seeded and minced

1 clove garlic, minced

⅛ teaspoon ground allspice

1 cup chicken broth

1 large sweet potato, peeled and cut into ¾-inch pieces

1 cup thawed frozen corn

1 tablespoon lime juice

Hot cooked rice (optional)

Jalapeño peppers can sting and irritate the skin, so wear rubber gloves when handling and do not touch your eyes.

1 Combine flour, salt and black pepper in large resealable food storage bag. Add pork; shake to coat. Press Sauté; heat oil in Instant Pot. Add pork in two batches, cook about 5 minutes or until browned. Remove to plate.

2 Add 2 tablespoons green onions, jalapeño, garlic and allspice to pot; cook and stir 30 seconds. Stir in broth, scraping up browned bits from bottom of pot. Return pork to pot.

3 Secure lid and move pressure release valve to Sealing position. Press Pressure Cook or Manual; cook at high pressure 18 minutes.

4 When cooking is complete, press Cancel and use quick release. Add sweet potato to pot. Secure lid and move pressure release valve to Sealing position. Press Pressure Cook or Manual; cook at high pressure 2 minutes.

5 When cooking is complete, press Cancel and use quick release.

6 Stir in corn, remaining 2 tablespoons green onions and lime juice; let stand 2 minutes or until corn is heated through. Serve with rice, if desired.

Beef Pot Pie
Makes 4 to 6 servings

⅓ cup all-purpose flour

1½ teaspoons salt, divided

½ teaspoon black pepper, divided

1½ pounds beef stew meat, cut into 1-inch pieces

2 tablespoons olive oil

¾ cup beef broth

½ cup stout, dark beer or ale

1 teaspoon chopped fresh thyme *or* ½ teaspoon dried thyme

1 pound unpeeled new red potatoes, cut into 1-inch pieces

2 cups baby carrots, halved crosswise

1 cup frozen pearl onions, thawed *or* 1 large onion, chopped

1 parsnip, peeled and cut into 1-inch pieces

1 refrigerated pie crust (half of 15-ounce package)

1 Combine flour, ½ teaspoon salt and ¼ teaspoon pepper in large resealable food storage bag. Add beef; toss to coat.

2 Press Sauté; heat oil in Instant Pot. Add beef in two batches; cook about 5 minutes or until browned. Stir in broth, stout, thyme, remaining 1 teaspoon salt and ¼ teaspoon pepper; mix well.

3 Secure lid and move pressure release valve to Sealing position. Press Pressure Cook or Manual; cook at high pressure 25 minutes.

4 When cooking is complete, press Cancel and use quick release. Add potatoes, carrots, onions and parsnip to pot; mix well. Secure lid and move pressure release valve to Sealing position. Press Pressure Cook or Manual; cook at high pressure 15 minutes. Meanwhile, remove pie crust from refrigerator; let stand at room temperature 15 minutes. Preheat oven to 425°F.

5 When cooking is complete, press Cancel and use quick release. Pour beef mixture into 2½- to 3-quart baking dish. Place pie crust over filling; press edges to seal. Cut slits in crust to vent.

6 Bake 15 to 20 minutes or until crust is golden brown. Cool slightly before serving.

Italian Tomato-Braised Lamb

Makes 4 servings

1 can (28 ounces) whole plum tomatoes, undrained

4 bone-in lamb shoulder chops (¾ to 1 inch thick, about 2 pounds)

1½ teaspoons dried oregano

½ teaspoon salt

¼ teaspoon black pepper

2 tablespoons olive oil

2 onions, cut into quarters and thinly sliced

3 cloves garlic, minced

2 tablespoons red wine vinegar

3 to 4 sprigs fresh rosemary

Hot cooked polenta or pasta (optional)

1 Drain tomatoes, reserving 1 cup juice. Coarsely chop tomatoes. (Tomatoes can also be broken up with hands or cut with scissors in can.)

2 Season both sides of lamb with oregano, salt and pepper. Press Sauté; heat oil in Instant Pot. Add onions and garlic; cook and stir 3 minutes or until softened. Add tomatoes, reserved 1 cup juice and vinegar; cook and stir 1 minute. Add lamb and rosemary to pot, pressing into liquid.

3 Secure lid and move pressure release valve to Sealing position. Press Pressure Cook or Manual; cook at high pressure 12 minutes.

4 When cooking is complete, use natural release for 10 minutes, then release remaining pressure. Remove lamb to plate; tent with foil. Remove and discard rosemary sprigs.

5 Press Sauté; cook 5 to 10 minutes or until sauce is reduced by one third. Serve sauce with lamb and polenta, if desired.

Chorizo Burritos

Makes 4 servings

15 ounces uncooked Mexican chorizo sausages, cut into bite-size pieces

2 green or red bell peppers, cut into 1-inch pieces

1 can (about 15 ounces) red beans, rinsed and drained

1 can (about 14 ounces) diced tomatoes

1 can (11 ounces) corn, drained

½ teaspoon ground cumin

½ teaspoon ground cinnamon

8 (8-inch) flour tortillas, warmed

2 cups hot cooked rice

Shredded Monterey Jack cheese

1 Combine chorizo, bell peppers, beans, tomatoes, corn, cumin and cinnamon in Instant Pot; mix well.

2 Secure lid and move pressure release valve to Sealing position. Press Pressure Cook or Manual; cook at high pressure 10 minutes.

3 When cooking is complete, use natural release for 10 minutes, then release remaining pressure.

4 Press Sauté; cook about 5 minutes or until chorizo mixture thickens, stirring occasionally.

5 Spoon chorizo mixture down centers of tortillas; top with rice and shredded cheese. Roll up tortillas; serve immediately.

Tex-Mex Chili

Makes 4 to 6 servings

4 slices bacon, chopped

⅓ cup all-purpose flour

1½ teaspoons salt, divided

¼ teaspoon black pepper

2 pounds boneless beef top round or chuck shoulder steak, cut into ½-inch pieces

1 medium onion, chopped, plus additional for garnish

2 cloves garlic, minced

1¼ cups water

¼ cup chili powder

1 teaspoon dried oregano

1 teaspoon ground cumin

½ to 1 teaspoon ground red pepper

½ teaspoon hot pepper sauce

1 Press Sauté; cook bacon in Instant Pot until crisp. Remove to paper towel-lined plate.

2 Combine flour, ½ teaspoon salt and black pepper in large resealable food storage bag. Add beef; toss to coat. Add beef to bacon drippings in two batches; cook about 5 minutes or until browned. Remove to plate.

3 Add onion to pot; cook and stir 3 minutes or until softened. Add garlic; cook and stir 1 minute. Return beef and bacon to pot. Add water, chili powder, remaining 1 teaspoon salt, oregano, cumin, red pepper and hot pepper sauce; cook and stir 2 minutes, scraping up browned bits from bottom of pot.

4 Secure lid and move pressure release valve to Sealing position. Press Pressure Cook or Manual; cook at high pressure 20 minutes.

5 When cooking is complete, use natural release for 10 minutes, then release remaining pressure. Serve with additional chopped onion, if desired.

Tip

Texas chili doesn't contain any beans. But if you want to stretch this recipe and dilute some of the spiciness—and you don't live in Texas!—you can add canned pinto beans to the chili after the pressure has been released. Press Sauté and cook until the beans are heated through.

Honey Ginger Ribs

Makes 4 servings

2 pounds pork baby back ribs, trimmed and cut into 2-rib sections

4 green onions, chopped

½ cup hoisin sauce, divided

3 tablespoons dry sherry or rice wine

2 tablespoons honey

2 tablespoons soy sauce

1 tablespoon cider vinegar

1 tablespoon packed brown sugar

2 cloves garlic, minced

1 teaspoon minced fresh ginger

¼ teaspoon Chinese five-spice powder

⅓ cup chicken or beef broth

2 tablespoons cornstarch

Sesame seeds (optional)

1 Place ribs in large resealable food storage bag. Combine green onions, ¼ cup hoisin sauce, sherry, honey, soy sauce, vinegar, brown sugar, garlic, ginger and five-spice powder in medium bowl; mix well. Pour marinade over ribs. Seal bag; turn to coat. Refrigerate 2 to 4 hours or overnight, turning occasionally.

2 Pour broth into Instant Pot; add ribs and marinade. Secure lid and move pressure release valve to Sealing position. Press Pressure Cook or Manual; cook at high pressure 25 minutes.

3 When cooking is complete, use natural release for 10 minutes, then release remaining pressure. Remove ribs to plate; tent with foil.

4 Skim excess fat from surface of sauce. Place cornstarch in small bowl; stir in 2 tablespoons sauce until smooth. Press Sauté; add cornstarch mixture to pot, stirring constantly. Cook and stir about 2 minutes or until sauce thickens slightly. Add remaining ¼ cup hoisin sauce; cook and stir until heated through.

5 Brush sauce over ribs before serving. Sprinkle with sesame seeds, if desired.

Beef Stew with a Coffee Kick

Makes 6 servings

⅓ cup all-purpose flour

1 teaspoon salt

1 teaspoon dried marjoram

½ teaspoon garlic powder

½ teaspoon black pepper

2 pounds beef stew meat, cut into 1-inch pieces

2 tablespoons vegetable oil

3 small onions, cut into wedges

¾ cup strong brewed coffee, at room temperature

1 can (about 14 ounces) diced tomatoes

1 bay leaf

2 cups diced peeled potatoes (½-inch pieces)

4 stalks celery, cut into ½-inch slices

4 medium carrots, cut into ½-inch slices

1 Combine flour, salt, marjoram, garlic powder and pepper in large resealable food storage bag. Add beef; toss to coat.

2 Press Sauté; heat oil in Instant Pot. Add beef in two batches; cook about 5 minutes or until browned. Remove to plate.

3 Add onions to pot; cook and stir 3 minutes or until softened. Add coffee; cook and stir 1 minute, scraping up browned bits from bottom of pot. Return beef to pot with tomatoes and bay leaf; mix well.

4 Secure lid and move pressure release valve to Sealing position. Press Pressure Cook or Manual; cook at high pressure 25 minutes.

5 When cooking is complete, use natural release for 5 minutes, then release remaining pressure. Add potatoes, celery and carrots to pot. Secure lid and move pressure release valve to Sealing position. Press Pressure Cook or Manual; cook at high pressure 12 minutes.

6 When cooking is complete, press Cancel and use quick release. Remove and discard bay leaf. Let stew cool in pot 5 minutes, stirring occasionally. (Stew will thicken as it cools.)

Pork Picadillo

Makes 4 servings

1 tablespoon olive oil

1 pound boneless pork country-style ribs, trimmed and cut into ½-inch pieces

1 onion, chopped

2 cloves garlic, minced

1 can (about 14 ounces) diced tomatoes

½ cup raisins

2 tablespoons cider vinegar

2 canned chipotle peppers in adobo sauce, chopped

½ teaspoon salt

½ teaspoon ground cumin

½ teaspoon ground cinnamon

1 Press Sauté; heat oil in Instant Pot. Add pork; cook about 6 minutes or until browned, stirring occasionally. Add onion; cook and stir 2 minutes. Add garlic; cook and stir 30 seconds.

2 Stir in tomatoes, raisins, vinegar, chipotle peppers, salt, cumin and cinnamon, scraping up browned bits from bottom of pot.

3 Secure lid and move pressure release valve to Sealing position. Press Pressure Cook or Manual; cook at high pressure 25 minutes.

4 When cooking is complete, use natural release for 10 minutes, then release remaining pressure. Stir pork mixture with tongs, breaking up pork into smaller pieces.

Corned Beef and Cabbage

Makes 3 to 4 servings

1 corned beef brisket
   (3 to 4 pounds) with
   seasoning packet

2 cups water

1 head cabbage (1½ pounds),
   cut into 6 wedges

1 package (16 ounces) baby
   carrots

1 Place corned beef in Instant Pot, fat side up; sprinkle with seasoning. Pour water into pot.

2 Secure lid and move pressure release valve to Sealing position. Press Pressure Cook or Manual; cook at high pressure 90 minutes.

3 When cooking is complete, use natural release for 10 minutes, then release remaining pressure. Remove beef to cutting board; tent with foil.

4 Add cabbage and carrots to pot. Secure lid and move pressure release valve to Sealing position. Press Pressure Cook or Manual; cook at high pressure 4 minutes. When cooking is complete, press Cancel and use quick release.

5 Slice beef; serve with vegetables.

Canton Pork Stew

Makes 6 servings

1 cup chicken broth
¼ cup dry sherry
3 tablespoons soy sauce
1 tablespoon hoisin sauce
1½ tablespoons cornstarch
2 tablespoons vegetable oil
1½ pounds boneless pork shoulder, trimmed and cut into 1-inch pieces
1 large onion, chopped
3 cloves garlic, minced
1 teaspoon Chinese five-spice powder
½ teaspoon salt
2 cups baby carrots
1 large green bell pepper, cut into 1-inch pieces

1 Combine broth, sherry, soy sauce and hoisin sauce in medium bowl; mix well. Stir 3 tablespoons broth mixture into cornstarch in small bowl until smooth; set aside.

2 Press Sauté; heat oil in Instant Pot. Add pork in two batches; cook about 5 minutes or until browned. Remove to plate.

3 Add onion to pot; cook and stir 3 minutes or until softened. Add garlic, five-spice powder and salt; cook and stir 30 seconds. Add broth mixture; cook and stir 1 minute, scraping up browned bits from bottom of pot. Return pork to pot.

4 Secure lid and move pressure release valve to Sealing position. Press Pressure Cook or Manual; cook at high pressure 15 minutes.

5 When cooking is complete, press Cancel and use quick release. Add carrots and bell pepper to pot. Secure lid and move pressure release valve to Sealing position. Press Pressure Cook or Manual; cook at high pressure 2 minutes. When cooking is complete, press Cancel and use quick release.

6 Stir reserved cornstarch mixture. Press Sauté; add cornstarch mixture to pot, stirring constantly. Cook and stir about 1 minute or until stew thickens.

Mole Chili

Makes 4 servings

2 tablespoons olive oil, divided

1½ pounds boneless beef chuck, cut into 1-inch pieces

2 medium onions, chopped

5 cloves garlic, minced

1 cup beef broth, divided

1 can (about 14 ounces) fire-roasted diced tomatoes

2 corn tortillas, each cut into 4 wedges

2 tablespoons chili powder

1 tablespoon ancho chili powder

1 teaspoon dried oregano

1 teaspoon ground cumin

¾ teaspoon salt

¾ teaspoon ground cinnamon

½ teaspoon black pepper

1 can (about 15 ounces) red kidney beans, rinsed and drained

1½ ounces semisweet chocolate, chopped

1 Press Sauté; heat 1 tablespoon oil in Instant Pot. Add beef in two batches; cook about 5 minutes or until browned. Remove to plate. Add remaining 1 tablespoon oil, onions and garlic to pot; cook and stir about 3 minutes or until softened. Stir in ½ cup broth, scraping up browned bits from bottom of pot. Stir in remaining ½ cup broth, beef, tomatoes, tortillas, chili powders, oregano, cumin, salt, cinnamon and pepper; mix well.

2 Secure lid and move pressure release valve to Sealing position. Press Pressure Cook or Manual; cook at high pressure 30 minutes.

3 When cooking is complete, use natural release for 15 minutes, then release remaining pressure.

4 Press Sauté; add beans and chocolate to pot. Cook and stir 2 minutes or until chocolate is melted and beans are heated through.

Beer Barbecued Pulled Pork Sandwiches

Makes 8 servings

1 tablespoon chili powder

½ teaspoon salt

¼ teaspoon black pepper

2 pounds boneless pork shoulder, trimmed and cut into 3-inch pieces

1 tablespoon vegetable oil

1 cup chopped onion

½ cup ale or dark beer*

⅓ cup ketchup

¼ cup chicken broth

3 tablespoons honey

2 tablespoons cider vinegar

2 tablespoons whole grain mustard

8 sandwich rolls, split

Bread-and-butter pickle chips

For best flavor, do not use light beer.

1 Combine chili powder, salt and pepper in small bowl; mix well. Rub spice mixture into all sides of pork.

2 Press Sauté; heat oil in Instant Pot. Add pork in batches; cook about 8 minutes or until browned on all sides. Remove to plate. Add onion, beer, ketchup, broth, honey, vinegar and mustard to pot; cook and stir 2 minutes, scraping up browned bits from bottom of pot. Return pork to pot, pressing into liquid.

3 Secure lid and move pressure release valve to Sealing position. Press Pressure Cook or Manual; cook at high pressure 45 minutes.

4 When cooking is complete, use natural release for 10 minutes, then release remaining pressure. Remove pork to clean plate.

5 Skim excess fat from surface of sauce. Press Sauté; cook about 10 minutes or until sauce is reduced by one third. Meanwhile, shred pork into bite-size pieces when cool enough to handle.

6 Combine pork and 1 cup sauce in large bowl; toss to coat. Add additional sauce if necessary. Serve on rolls with pickles.

Irish Beef Stew

Makes 6 servings

2½ tablespoons vegetable oil, divided

2 pounds boneless beef chuck roast, cut into 1-inch pieces

1½ teaspoons salt, divided

¾ teaspoon black pepper, divided

1 package (8 to 10 ounces) cremini mushrooms, quartered

1 medium onion, quartered

1 cup Guinness stout

1 tablespoon Dijon mustard

1 tablespoon tomato paste

1 tablespoon Worcestershire sauce

2 cloves garlic, minced

2 bay leaves

1 teaspoon dried thyme

1 teaspoon dried rosemary

1 pound small yellow potatoes (about 1¼ inches), halved

3 medium carrots, cut into ¾-inch pieces

3 medium parsnips, cut into ¾-inch pieces

2 teaspoons water

2 teaspoons cornstarch

1 cup frozen pearl onions

Chopped fresh parsley (optional)

1 Press Sauté; heat 2 tablespoons oil in Instant Pot. Season beef with 1 teaspoon salt and ½ teaspoon pepper. Cook beef in two batches about 5 minutes or until browned. Remove to plate.

2 Add remaining ½ tablespoon oil, mushrooms and onion quarters to pot; cook about 6 minutes or until mushrooms release their liquid and begin to brown, stirring frequently. Add Guinness, mustard, tomato paste, Worcestershire sauce, garlic, bay leaves, thyme, rosemary, remaining ½ teaspoon salt and ¼ teaspoon pepper; cook and stir 3 minutes, scraping up browned bits from bottom of pot. Return beef and any accumulated juices to pot; mix well.

3 Secure lid and move pressure release valve to Sealing position. Press Pressure Cook or Manual; cook at high pressure 30 minutes.

4 When cooking is complete, press Cancel and use quick release. Remove and discard bay leaves and large onion pieces. Add potatoes, carrots and parsnips to pot; mix well. Secure lid and move pressure release valve to Sealing position. Press Pressure Cook or Manual; cook at high pressure 3 minutes. Meanwhile, stir water into cornstarch in small bowl until smooth.

5 When cooking is complete, press Cancel and use quick release. Press Sauté; stir pearl onions into stew. Add cornstarch mixture; cook 2 to 3 minutes or until stew thickens, stirring frequently. Garnish with parsley.

Easy Meatballs

Makes 4 servings

1 pound ground beef

1 egg, beaten

3 tablespoons Italian-
    seasoned dry
    bread crumbs

1 clove garlic, minced

1 teaspoon dried oregano

¾ teaspoon salt

¼ teaspoon black pepper

⅛ teaspoon ground red
    pepper

3 cups marinara or tomato-
    basil pasta sauce

   Hot cooked spaghetti

   Chopped fresh basil
   (optional)

   Grated Parmesan cheese
   (optional)

1 Combine beef, egg, bread crumbs, garlic, oregano, salt, black pepper and red pepper in medium bowl; mix gently. Shape into 16 (1½-inch) meatballs.

2 Pour pasta sauce into Instant Pot. Add meatballs to sauce; turn to coat and submerge meatballs in sauce.

3 Secure lid and move pressure release valve to Sealing position. Press Pressure Cook or Manual; cook at high pressure 8 minutes.

4 When cooking is complete, press Cancel and use quick release. Serve meatballs and sauce over spaghetti; top with basil and cheese, if desired.

Lamb and Chickpea Stew

Makes 4 to 6 servings

- 1 cup dried chickpeas, soaked 8 hours or overnight
- 2 tablespoons vegetable oil, divided
- 1 pound lamb stew meat
- 1 large onion, chopped
- 1 tablespoon minced garlic
- 1½ teaspoons salt
- 1½ teaspoons ground cumin
- 1 teaspoon ground turmeric
- 1 teaspoon ground coriander
- 1 teaspoon ground cinnamon
- ¼ teaspoon black pepper
- 1 can (about 14 ounces) diced tomatoes
- 1½ cups chicken broth
- ½ cup chopped dried apricots, divided
- ¼ cup chopped fresh Italian parsley
- 2 tablespoons lemon juice
- 1 tablespoon honey
  Hot cooked couscous

1 Drain and rinse chickpeas. Press Sauté; heat 1 tablespoon oil in Instant Pot. Add lamb; cook 6 minutes or until browned, stirring occasionally. Add remaining 1 tablespoon oil and onion to pot; cook and stir 3 minutes or until softened. Add garlic, salt, cumin, turmeric, coriander, cinnamon and pepper; cook and stir 1 minute. Add tomatoes and broth; cook and stir 2 minutes, scraping up browned bits from bottom of pot. Stir in chickpeas and half of apricots; mix well.

2 Secure lid and move pressure release valve to Sealing position. Press Pressure Cook or Manual; cook at high pressure 20 minutes.

3 When cooking is complete, use natural release for 10 minutes, then release remaining pressure.

4 Press Sauté; add remaining half of apricots to pot. Cook 5 minutes or until sauce is reduced and thickens slightly, stirring frequently. Stir in parsley, lemon juice and honey. Serve with couscous.

SEAFOOD

Sea Bass with Vegetables

Makes 6 servings

- 2 tablespoons butter or olive oil
- 2 bulbs fennel, thinly sliced
- 3 large carrots, julienned
- 3 large leeks, thinly sliced
- ¾ teaspoon salt, divided
- ¼ teaspoon plus ⅛ teaspoon black pepper, divided
- 6 sea bass fillets or other firm-fleshed white fish (6 to 8 ounces each)
- ¼ cup water

1 Press Sauté; melt butter in Instant Pot. Add fennel, carrots and leeks; cook about 8 minutes or until vegetables are softened and beginning to brown, stirring occasionally. Stir in ½ teaspoon salt and ¼ teaspoon pepper. Remove half of vegetables to plate.

2 Season sea bass with remaining ¼ teaspoon salt and ⅛ teaspoon pepper; place on top of vegetables in pot. Top with remaining vegetables. Drizzle with water.

3 Secure lid and move pressure release valve to Sealing position. Press Pressure Cook or Manual; cook at low pressure 4 minutes.

4 When cooking is complete, press Cancel and use quick release. Serve fish with vegetables.

Italian Fish Soup

Makes 4 servings

1 can (about 14 ounces)
   Italian-seasoned
   diced tomatoes

1 cup chicken broth

1 small bulb fennel, chopped
   (about 1 cup), fronds
   reserved for garnish

3 cloves garlic, minced

1 tablespoon olive oil

½ teaspoon saffron threads,
   crushed (optional)

½ teaspoon dried basil

¼ teaspoon salt

¼ teaspoon red pepper flakes

8 ounces skinless halibut
   or cod fillets, cut into
   1-inch pieces

8 ounces medium raw shrimp,
   peeled and deveined

1 Combine tomatoes, broth, chopped fennel, garlic, oil, saffron, if desired, basil, salt and red pepper flakes in Instant Pot; mix well.

2 Secure lid and move pressure release valve to Sealing position. Press Pressure Cook or Manual; cook at high pressure 3 minutes. When cooking is complete, press Cancel and use quick release.

3 Add halibut to pot. Secure lid and move pressure release valve to Sealing position. Press Pressure Cook or Manual; cook at low pressure 1 minute.

4 When cooking is complete, press Cancel and use quick release.

5 Press Sauté; add shrimp to pot. Cook 2 to 3 minutes or until shrimp are pink and opaque, stirring occasionally. Garnish with fennel fronds.

Cod with Tapenade

Makes 4 servings

Tapenade (recipe follows)
4 cod fillets or other firm
     white fish (about
     8 ounces each)
¼ teaspoon salt
⅛ teaspoon black pepper
1 cup water
2 lemons, thinly sliced

1 Prepare Tapenade.

2 Season cod with salt and pepper. Pour water into Instant Pot. Place rack in pot; arrange half of lemon slices on rack. Place cod on lemon slices; top with remaining lemon slices.

3 Secure lid and move pressure release valve to Sealing position. Press Pressure Cook or Manual; cook at low pressure 2 minutes.

4 When cooking is complete, press Cancel and use quick release. Remove fish to serving plates; discard lemon slices. Serve with Tapenade.

Tapenade

Makes about 1 cup

8 ounces pitted kalamata
     olives
2 tablespoons anchovy paste
2 tablespoons drained
     capers
2 tablespoons chopped
     fresh Italian parsley
1 clove garlic
½ teaspoon grated
     orange peel
⅛ teaspoon ground
     red pepper
½ cup extra virgin olive oil

Combine olives, anchovy paste, capers, parsley, garlic, orange peel and red pepper in food processor; pulse until coarsely chopped. Add oil; pulse until mixture forms rough paste. (Tapenade should not be completely smooth.)

Shrimp Jambalaya

Makes 6 servings

2 cans (about 14 ounces each) diced tomatoes, drained

1 medium onion, chopped

1 medium red bell pepper, chopped

1 stalk celery, chopped

2 tablespoons minced garlic

2 teaspoons dried parsley flakes

2 teaspoons dried oregano

1 teaspoon salt

1 teaspoon hot pepper sauce

½ teaspoon dried thyme

2 pounds medium raw shrimp, peeled and deveined

Hot cooked rice

1 Combine tomatoes, onion, bell pepper, celery, garlic, parsley flakes, oregano, salt, hot pepper sauce and thyme in Instant Pot; mix well.

2 Secure lid and move pressure release valve to Sealing position. Press Pressure Cook or Manual; cook at high pressure 9 minutes.

3 When cooking is complete, press Cancel and use quick release.

4 Press Sauté; add shrimp to pot. Cook 5 minutes or until shrimp are pink and opaque and jambalaya is slightly reduced. Serve over rice.

Greek-Style Salmon

Makes 4 servings

1 tablespoon olive oil

1 can (about 14 ounces) diced
   tomatoes, drained

¼ cup pitted black olives,
   coarsely chopped

¼ cup pitted green olives,
   coarsely chopped

3 tablespoons lemon juice

2 tablespoons chopped
   fresh Italian parsley

1 tablespoon capers,
   rinsed and drained

2 cloves garlic, thinly sliced

¼ teaspoon black pepper

1 pound salmon fillets

1 Press Sauté; heat oil in Instant Pot. Add tomatoes, olives, lemon juice, parsley, capers, garlic and pepper; bring to a simmer, stirring frequently.

2 Secure lid and move pressure release valve to Sealing position. Press Pressure Cook or Manual; cook at high pressure 4 minutes.

3 When cooking is complete, press Cancel and use quick release.

4 Place salmon in pot, skin side down. Press Sauté; bring to a simmer. Turn off heat; cover pot with lid and let stand 10 minutes or until fish begins to flake when tested with fork.

Tortilla Soup with Grouper

Makes 6 servings

1 tablespoon vegetable oil

1 onion, chopped

2 cloves garlic, minced

3½ cups chicken broth

1 can (about 14 ounces) diced tomatoes

1 can (4 ounces) diced green chiles, drained

2 teaspoons Worcestershire sauce

1 teaspoon salt

1 teaspoon chili powder

1 teaspoon ground cumin

⅛ teaspoon black pepper

1 pound grouper or sole fillets, cut into 1-inch pieces

1 cup frozen corn

3 corn tortillas, cut into 1-inch strips

1 Press Sauté; heat oil in Instant Pot. Add onion and garlic; cook and stir 3 minutes or until onion is softened. Add broth, tomatoes, chiles, Worcestershire sauce, salt, chili powder, cumin and pepper; mix well.

2 Secure lid and move pressure release valve to Sealing position. Press Pressure Cook or Manual; cook at high pressure 4 minutes.

3 When cooking is complete, press Cancel and use quick release.

4 Press Sauté; add grouper and corn to pot. Cook about 2 minutes or until fish begins to flake when tested with fork. Stir in tortillas; serve immediately.

Scallops with Herb Tomato Sauce

Makes 4 servings

2 tablespoons vegetable oil

1 medium red onion, peeled and diced

1 clove garlic, minced

3½ cups fresh tomatoes, peeled*

1 can (6 ounces) tomato paste

¼ cup dry red wine

2 tablespoons chopped fresh Italian parsley

1 tablespoon chopped fresh oregano

1 teaspoon salt

¼ teaspoon black pepper

1½ pounds fresh scallops, cleaned and drained

Hot cooked pasta or rice (optional)

*To peel tomatoes, score "x" in bottom of tomatoes and place one at a time in simmering water about 10 seconds. (Add 30 seconds if tomatoes are not fully ripened.) Immediately plunge into bowl of cold water for another 10 seconds. Peel skin with a knife.

1 Press Sauté; heat oil in Instant Pot. Add onion and garlic; cook and stir 4 minutes or until onion is translucent. Add tomatoes, tomato paste, wine, parsley, oregano, 1 teaspoon salt and ¼ teaspoon pepper; mix well.

2 Secure lid and move pressure release valve to Sealing position. Press Pressure Cook or Manual; cook at high pressure 8 minutes.

3 When cooking is complete, press Cancel and use quick release. Taste sauce; season with additional salt and pepper if necessary.

4 Press Sauté; add scallops to pot. Cook 1 minute or until sauce begins to simmer. Press Cancel; cover pot with lid and let stand 8 minutes or until scallops are opaque. Serve with pasta, if desired.

Cod Chowder

Makes 6 to 8 servings

2 tablespoons vegetable oil

1 pound unpeeled red potatoes, diced

2 medium leeks, halved and thinly sliced

2 stalks celery, diced

1 bulb fennel, diced

½ yellow or red bell pepper, diced

2 teaspoons chopped fresh thyme

1¼ teaspoons salt

½ teaspoon black pepper

2 tablespoons all-purpose flour

2 cups clam juice

1 cup water

1½ pounds cod, cut into 1-inch pieces

1 cup frozen corn

1 cup half-and-half

¼ cup finely chopped fresh Italian parsley

1 Press Sauté; heat oil in Instant Pot. Add potatoes, leeks, celery, fennel, bell pepper, thyme, salt and black pepper; cook about 8 minutes or until vegetables are slightly softened, stirring occasionally. Add flour; cook and stir 1 minute. Add clam juice and water; mix well.

2 Secure lid and move pressure release valve to Sealing position. Press Pressure Cook or Manual; cook at high pressure 6 minutes.

3 When cooking is complete, press Cancel and use quick release. Use immersion blender to blend soup just until slightly thickened but still chunky (soup should not be completely smooth).

4 Press Sauté; add cod, corn, half-and-half and parsley to pot. Cook about 2 minutes or until soup begins to simmer and fish is firm and opaque, stirring occasionally.

Shrimp and Okra Gumbo

Makes 6 servings

1 tablespoon olive oil

8 ounces kielbasa sausage, halved lengthwise then cut crosswise into ¼-inch slices

1 green bell pepper, chopped

1 medium onion, chopped

3 stalks celery, cut into ¼-inch slices

6 green onions, chopped

4 cloves garlic, minced

1 can (about 14 ounces) diced tomatoes

½ cup chicken broth

1 teaspoon Cajun seasoning

½ teaspoon dried thyme

¼ teaspoon salt

2 cups frozen cut okra, thawed

1 pound large raw shrimp, peeled and deveined (with tails on)

1 Press Sauté; heat oil in Instant Pot. Add kielbasa; cook and stir 4 minutes or until browned. Remove to plate.

2 Add bell pepper, chopped onion, celery, green onions and garlic to pot; cook and stir 6 minutes or until vegetables are softened. Stir in kielbasa, tomatoes, broth, Cajun seasoning, thyme and salt; mix well.

3 Secure lid and move pressure release valve to Sealing position. Press Pressure Cook or Manual; cook at high pressure 4 minutes.

4 When cooking is complete, press Cancel and use quick release.

5 Add okra to pot. Secure lid and move pressure release valve to Sealing position. Press Pressure Cook or Manual; cook at high pressure 1 minute. When cooking is complete, press Cancel and use quick release.

6 Press Sauté; add shrimp to pot. Cook 2 to 3 minutes or until shrimp are pink and opaque, stirring occasionally.

Southwestern Salmon Po' Boys

Makes 4 servings

½ teaspoon Southwest seasoning or chipotle chili powder

¼ teaspoon salt

¼ teaspoon black pepper

4 salmon fillets (about 6 ounces each), rinsed and patted dry

1 red bell pepper, thinly sliced

1 green bell pepper, thinly sliced

1 onion, thinly sliced

½ cup Italian vinaigrette dressing

¼ cup water

4 large French or Italian sandwich rolls, split

¼ cup chipotle mayonnaise*

Fresh cilantro leaves (optional)

½ lemon, cut into 4 wedges

If unavailable, combine ¼ cup mayonnaise with ½ teaspoon adobo sauce. Or substitute regular mayonnaise.

1 Combine Southwest seasoning, salt and black pepper in small bowl; mix well. Rub spice mixture over both sides of salmon.

2 Combine half of bell peppers and half of onion in Instant Pot. Place salmon on top of vegetables. Pour Italian dressing over salmon; top with remaining bell peppers and onion. Pour water into pot.

3 Secure lid and move pressure release valve to Sealing position. Press Pressure Cook or Manual; cook at low pressure 4 minutes.

4 When cooking is complete, press Cancel and use quick release. Remove salmon to plate; remove and discard skin.

5 Toast rolls, if desired. Spread top halves with chipotle mayonnaise and cilantro, if desired. Spoon 1 to 2 tablespoons cooking liquid onto bottom halves of rolls; top with warm salmon, vegetable mixture and top halves of rolls. Serve with lemon wedges.

Savory Cod Stew

Makes 6 to 8 servings

8 ounces bacon, chopped
1 large onion, diced
1 large carrot, diced
2 stalks celery, diced
2 cloves garlic, minced
1 can (28 ounces) plum
   tomatoes, undrained,
   coarsely chopped
2 potatoes, peeled and diced
1 cup clam juice
3 tablespoons tomato paste
3 tablespoons chopped
   fresh Italian parsley
½ teaspoon salt
¼ teaspoon black pepper
3 saffron threads
2½ pounds fresh cod, skin
   removed, cut into
   1½-inch pieces

1 Press Sauté; cook bacon in Instant Pot until crisp. Drain off all but 2 tablespoons drippings.

2 Add onion, carrot, celery and garlic to pot; cook and stir 5 minutes or until vegetables are softened. Add tomatoes with juice, potatoes, clam juice, tomato paste, parsley, salt, pepper and saffron; cook and stir 2 minutes.

3 Secure lid and move pressure release valve to Sealing position. Press Pressure Cook or Manual; cook at high pressure 2 minutes.

4 When cooking is complete, press Cancel and use quick release.

5 Add cod to pot. Secure lid and move pressure release valve to Sealing position. Press Pressure Cook or Manual; cook at low pressure 1 minute.

6 When cooking is complete, press Cancel and use quick release.

VEGETABLES

Sweet and Sour Red Cabbage

Makes 8 servings

- 2 slices thick-cut bacon, chopped
- 1 cup chopped onion
- 1 head red cabbage (2 to 3 pounds), thinly sliced (about 8 cups)
- 1 pound unpeeled Granny Smith apples, cut into ½-inch pieces (about 2 medium)
- ½ cup honey
- ½ cup cider vinegar
- ¼ cup plus 3 tablespoons water, divided
- 1 teaspoon salt
- 1 teaspoon celery salt
- ¼ teaspoon black pepper
- 2 tablespoons all-purpose flour

1 Press Sauté, cook bacon in Instant Pot until crisp. Remove to paper towel-lined plate.

2 Add onion to pot; cook and stir 3 minutes or until softened. Stir in cabbage, apples, honey, vinegar, ¼ cup water, salt, celery salt and pepper; mix well.

3 Secure lid and move pressure release valve to Sealing position. Press Pressure Cook or Manual; cook at high pressure 5 minutes.

4 When cooking is complete, use natural release for 10 minutes, then release remaining pressure.

5 Stir remaining 3 tablespoons water into flour in small bowl until smooth. Press Sauté; add flour mixture to pot. Cook and stir about 3 minutes or until sauce thickens. Sprinkle with bacon; serve warm.

Lemon-Mint Red Potatoes

Makes 4 servings

2 pounds unpeeled new red potatoes (1½ to 2 inches)

⅓ cup water

4 tablespoons chopped fresh mint, divided

1 tablespoon olive oil

1 teaspoon salt

1 teaspoon grated lemon peel

¾ teaspoon Greek seasoning or dried oregano

¼ teaspoon black pepper

1 tablespoon lemon juice

1 tablespoon butter

1 Combine potatoes, water, 2 tablespoons mint, oil, salt, lemon peel, Greek seasoning and pepper in Instant Pot; mix well.

2 Secure lid and move pressure release valve to Sealing position. Press Pressure Cook or Manual; cook at high pressure 6 minutes.

3 When cooking is complete, press Cancel and use quick release.

4 Press Sauté; add remaining 2 tablespoons mint, lemon juice and butter to pot. Cook and stir 2 minutes or until butter is melted and potatoes are completely coated.

Shakshuka

Makes 4 servings

- 2 tablespoons extra virgin olive oil
- 1 large red bell pepper, chopped
- 1 medium onion, chopped
- 3 cloves garlic, minced
- 2 teaspoons sugar
- 2 teaspoons ground cumin
- 1 teaspoon paprika
- 1 teaspoon chili powder
- ½ teaspoon salt
- ¼ teaspoon red pepper flakes
- 1 can (28 ounces) crushed tomatoes
- ¾ cup crumbled feta cheese
- 4 eggs

1 Press Sauté; heat oil in Instant Pot. Add bell pepper and onion; cook and stir 3 minutes or until softened. Add garlic, sugar, cumin, paprika, chili powder, salt and red pepper flakes to pot; cook and stir 1 minute. Stir in tomatoes; mix well.

2 Secure lid and move pressure release valve to Sealing position. Press Pressure Cook or Manual; cook at high pressure 10 minutes.

3 When cooking is complete, press Cancel and use quick release.

4 Stir in cheese. Make four wells in sauce for eggs, leaving space between each. Slide eggs, one at a time, into wells in sauce. (For best results, crack each egg into small bowl before sliding into sauce.)

5 Secure lid and move pressure release valve to Sealing position. Press Pressure Cook or Manual; cook at low pressure 1 minute. When cooking is complete, press Cancel and use quick release. To cook eggs longer, press Sauté and cook until desired doneness.

Spiced Sweet Potatoes

Makes 4 to 6 servings

2½ pounds sweet potatoes,
     peeled and cut into
     ½-inch pieces

½ cup water

2 tablespoons dark brown
   sugar

1 teaspoon salt

1 teaspoon ground cinnamon

½ teaspoon ground nutmeg

2 tablespoons butter, cut
   into small pieces

½ teaspoon vanilla

1 Combine sweet potatoes, water, brown sugar, salt, cinnamon and nutmeg in Instant Pot; mix well.

2 Secure lid and move pressure release valve to Sealing position. Press Pressure Cook or Manual; cook at high pressure 3 minutes.

3 When cooking is complete, press Cancel and use quick release.

4 Press Sauté; add butter and vanilla to pot. Cook 1 to 2 minutes or until butter is melted, stirring gently to blend.

Eggplant Italiano

Makes 6 servings

- 1 tablespoon olive oil
- 2 medium onions, thinly sliced
- 1¼ pounds eggplant, cut into 1-inch cubes
- 2 medium stalks celery, cut into 1-inch pieces
- 1 can (about 14 ounces) diced tomatoes
- ½ cup pitted black olives, sliced
- 3 tablespoons tomato sauce
- 2 tablespoons balsamic vinegar
- 1 tablespoon sugar
- 1 tablespoon capers, drained
- 1 teaspoon dried oregano or basil
- ¾ teaspoon salt
- ¼ teaspoon black pepper

1 Press Sauté; heat oil in Instant Pot. Add onions; cook and stir 3 minutes or until softened. Add eggplant, celery, tomatoes, olives, tomato sauce, vinegar, sugar, capers, oregano, salt and pepper; mix well.

2 Secure lid and move pressure release valve to Sealing position. Press Pressure Cook or Manual; cook at high pressure 2 minutes.

3 When cooking is complete, press Cancel and use quick release.

Warm Potato Salad

Makes 6 to 8 servings

2 pounds fingerling potatoes

¾ cup water

3 slices thick-cut bacon, cut into ½-inch pieces

1 small onion, diced

2 tablespoons olive oil

¼ cup cider vinegar

2 tablespoons capers, drained and rinsed

1 tablespoon Dijon mustard

¾ teaspoon salt

¼ teaspoon black pepper

⅓ cup chopped fresh parsley

1 Combine potatoes and water in Instant Pot. Secure lid and move pressure release valve to Sealing position. Press Pressure Cook or Manual; cook on high pressure 4 minutes.

2 When cooking is complete, press Cancel and use quick release. Drain potatoes; let stand until cool enough to handle. Dry out pot with paper towels.

3 Press Sauté; cook bacon in pot until crisp. Drain on paper towel-lined plate. Drain off all but 1 tablespoon drippings from pot. Adjust heat to low ("less"). Add onion and oil to pot; cook about 10 minutes or until onion begins to turn golden, stirring occasionally. Meanwhile, cut potatoes crosswise into ½-inch slices.

4 Add vinegar, capers, mustard, salt and pepper to pot; mix well. Turn off heat; stir in potatoes. Add parsley and bacon; stir gently to coat.

Balsamic Green Beans with Almonds

Makes 4 servings

1 cup water

1 pound fresh green beans, trimmed

1 tablespoon extra virgin olive oil

2 teaspoons balsamic vinegar

½ teaspoon salt

¼ teaspoon black pepper

2 tablespoons sliced almonds, toasted*

To toast almonds, cook in small skillet over medium heat 1 to 2 minutes or until lightly browned, stirring frequently.

1 Pour water into Instant Pot. Place rack in pot; place beans on rack. (Arrange beans perpendicular to rack to prevent beans from falling through.)

2 Secure lid and move pressure release valve to Sealing position. Press Pressure Cook or Manual; cook at high pressure 2 minutes.

3 When cooking is complete, press Cancel and use quick release. Remove rack from pot; place beans in large bowl.

4 Add oil, vinegar, salt and pepper; toss to coat. Sprinkle with almonds just before serving.

Coconut Butternut Squash

Makes 4 to 6 servings

1 tablespoon butter

½ cup chopped onion

1 butternut squash (about 3 pounds), peeled and cut into 1-inch pieces

1 can (about 13 ounces) coconut milk, well shaken

1 to 2 tablespoons packed brown sugar, divided

1¼ teaspoons salt

½ teaspoon ground cinnamon

¼ teaspoon ground nutmeg

¼ teaspoon ground allspice

2 teaspoons grated fresh ginger

2 tablespoons lemon juice

1 Press Sauté; melt butter in Instant Pot. Add onion; cook and stir 2 minutes. Add squash, coconut milk, 1 tablespoon brown sugar, salt, cinnamon, nutmeg and allspice; mix well.

2 Secure lid and move pressure release valve to Sealing position. Press Pressure Cook or Manual; cook at high pressure 6 minutes.

3 When cooking is complete, press Cancel and use quick release.

4 Stir ginger into squash mixture. Use immersion blender to blend squash until smooth (or purée in food processor or blender). Stir in lemon juice. Sprinkle individual servings with remaining 1 tablespoon brown sugar, if desired.

Speedy Minestrone

Makes 6 to 8 servings

1 tablespoon olive oil
1 medium onion, chopped
3 medium carrots, chopped
3 stalks celery, chopped
2 cloves garlic, minced
1½ teaspoons salt
1 teaspoon Italian seasoning
¼ teaspoon black pepper
⅛ teaspoon red pepper flakes
4 cups vegetable broth
2 cans (about 15 ounces each) cannellini beans, rinsed and drained
2 russet potatoes (about 6 ounces each), peeled and cut into ½-inch pieces
1 can (about 14 ounces) diced tomatoes
1 bunch kale, stemmed and chopped (about 6 cups)
Shredded Parmesan cheese (optional)

1 Press Sauté; heat oil in Instant Pot. Add onion, carrots, celery and garlic; cook and stir 5 minutes or until vegetables are softened. Add salt, Italian seasoning, black pepper and red pepper flakes; cook and stir 1 minute. Stir in broth, beans, potatoes and tomatoes; mix well.

2 Secure lid and move pressure release valve to Sealing position. Press Pressure Cook or Manual; cook at high pressure 3 minutes.

3 When cooking is complete, press Cancel and use quick release.

4 Stir in kale. Secure lid and move pressure release valve to Sealing position. Press Pressure Cook or Manual; cook at high pressure 2 minutes.

5 When cooking is complete, use natural release for 5 minutes, then release remaining pressure. Serve with cheese, if desired.

Chunky Ranch Potatoes

Makes 8 servings

3 pounds unpeeled red potatoes, quartered

½ cup water

1 teaspoon salt

½ cup ranch dressing

½ cup grated Parmesan cheese

¼ cup minced fresh chives

1 Combine potatoes, water and salt in Instant Pot; mix well.

2 Secure lid and move pressure release valve to Sealing position. Press Pressure Cook or Manual; cook at high pressure 5 minutes.

3 When cooking is complete, press Cancel and use quick release.

4 Add ranch dressing, cheese and chives to pot; stir gently to coat, breaking potatoes into chunks.

Fall Vegetable Medley

Makes 6 servings

2 medium Yukon Gold potatoes, peeled and cut into ½-inch pieces

2 medium sweet potatoes, peeled and cut into ½-inch pieces

3 parsnips, peeled and cut into ½-inch pieces

1 bulb fennel, cut into ½-inch pieces

½ cup chopped fresh parsley

2 tablespoons butter, cut into small pieces

⅔ cup chicken or vegetable broth

2 teaspoons salt

½ teaspoon black pepper

1 Combine Yukon Gold potatoes, sweet potatoes, parsnips, fennel, parsley and butter in Instant Pot.

2 Combine broth, salt and pepper in measuring cup or small bowl; mix well. Pour over vegetables; stir gently to coat.

3 Secure lid and move pressure release valve to Sealing position. Press Pressure Cook or Manual; cook at high pressure 4 minutes.

4 When cooking is complete, press Cancel and use quick release.

5 Gently stir vegetables. If some liquid remains in bottom of pot, press Sauté and cook 2 to 3 minutes or until liquid has evaporated.

Cider Vinaigrette-Glazed Beets

Makes 6 servings

- 6 medium red and/or golden beets (about 3 pounds)
- 1 cup water
- 2 tablespoons cider vinegar
- 1 tablespoon extra virgin olive oil
- 1 teaspoon Dijon mustard
- ½ teaspoon packed brown sugar
- ¾ teaspoon salt
- ¼ teaspoon black pepper
- ⅓ cup crumbled blue cheese (optional)

1 Cut tops off beets, leaving at least 1 inch of stems. Scrub beets under cold running water with soft vegetable brush, being careful not to break skins. Pour 1 cup water into Instant Pot. Place rack in pot; place beets on rack (or use steamer basket to hold beets).

2 Secure lid and move pressure release valve to Sealing position. Press Pressure Cook or Manual; cook at high pressure 22 minutes.

3 When cooking is complete, use natural release for 10 minutes, then release remaining pressure. Check doneness by inserting paring knife into beets; knife should go in easily. If not, cook an additional 2 to 4 minutes.

4 Whisk vinegar, oil, mustard, brown sugar, salt and pepper in medium bowl until well blended.

5 When beets are cool enough to handle, peel off skins and trim root ends. Cut into wedges. Add warm beets to vinaigrette; toss gently to coat. Sprinkle with cheese, if desired. Serve warm or at room temperature.

Tip

The cooking time depends on the size of the beets, which can vary. If beets are not tender enough, secure lid and cook under pressure 2 to 4 minutes longer.

Parmesan Potato Wedges

Makes 4 to 6 servings

2 pounds unpeeled red potatoes (about 6 medium), cut into ½-inch wedges

½ cup water

¼ cup finely chopped onion

2 tablespoons butter, cut into small pieces

1¼ teaspoons salt

1 teaspoon dried oregano

¼ teaspoon black pepper

¼ cup grated Parmesan cheese

1 Combine potatoes, water, onion, butter, salt, oregano and pepper in Instant Pot; mix well.

2 Secure lid and move pressure release valve to Sealing position. Press Pressure Cook or Manual; cook at high pressure 3 minutes.

3 When cooking is complete, press Cancel and use quick release.

4 Transfer potatoes to serving platter; sprinkle with cheese.

Summer Squash Lasagna

Makes 4 to 6 servings

- 2 tablespoons olive oil
- 1 onion, chopped
- 1 medium zucchini, cut crosswise into ¼-inch slices
- 1 medium yellow squash, cut crosswise into ¼-inch slices
- 2 cloves garlic, minced
- 1 teaspoon salt, divided
- 1 cup ricotta cheese
- 1½ cups (6 ounces) shredded mozzarella cheese, divided
- ½ cup grated Parmesan cheese, divided
- ¼ cup plus 2 tablespoons chopped fresh basil, divided
- 1 egg
- ¼ teaspoon black pepper
- 2¼ cups marinara sauce
- 8 oven-ready (no-boil) lasagna noodles
- 1 cup water

1 Spray 7-inch springform pan with nonstick cooking spray; set aside. Heat oil in large skillet over medium-high heat. Add onion, zucchini and yellow squash; cook and stir about 5 minutes or until vegetables are softened and lightly browned. Add garlic and ½ teaspoon salt; cook and stir 30 seconds.

2 Combine ricotta, ¼ cup mozzarella, ¼ cup Parmesan, ¼ cup basil, egg, remaining ½ teaspoon salt and pepper in medium bowl; mix well.

3 Spread ¼ cup marinara sauce in bottom of prepared springform pan. Layer with 2 noodles, breaking to fit. Spread one third of ricotta mixture over noodles. Top with one third of vegetables, ¼ cup mozzarella and ½ cup sauce. Repeat layers twice. For final layer, top with remaining 2 noodles, ½ cup sauce, ½ cup mozzarella and ¼ cup Parmesan. Cover pan tightly with foil.

4 Pour water into Instant Pot. Place pan on rack; lower rack into pot. Secure lid and move pressure release valve to Sealing position. Press Pressure Cook or Manual; cook at high pressure 20 minutes.

5 When cooking is complete, use natural release. Carefully remove pan from pot. Remove foil.

6 If desired, preheat broiler and broil lasagna for 1 minute or until cheese is browned. Cool in pan 10 minutes. Remove side of pan; cut into squares or wedges. Sprinkle with remaining 2 tablespoons basil.

Thai Red Curry with Tofu

Makes 4 servings

2 tablespoons vegetable oil

5 medium shallots, thinly sliced (about 1½ cups)

3 tablespoons Thai red curry paste

1 teaspoon minced garlic

1 teaspoon grated fresh ginger

1 can (about 13 ounces) unsweetened coconut milk, well shaken

1 medium sweet potato, peeled and cut into 1-inch pieces

1 small eggplant or large zucchini, halved lengthwise, then cut crosswise into ½-inch slices

1½ tablespoons soy sauce

1 tablespoon packed brown sugar

1 package (14 to 16 ounces) extra firm tofu, cut into 1-inch pieces

1 red bell pepper, cut into ¼-inch strips

½ cup green beans (1-inch pieces)

¼ cup chopped fresh basil

2 tablespoons lime juice

Hot cooked rice (optional)

1 Press Sauté; heat oil in Instant Pot. Add shallots; cook and stir 2 minutes or until softened. Add curry paste, garlic and ginger; cook and stir 1 minute. Stir in coconut milk, sweet potato, eggplant, soy sauce and brown sugar; mix well.

2 Secure lid and move pressure release valve to Sealing position. Press Pressure Cook or Manual; cook at high pressure 4 minutes.

3 When cooking is complete, press Cancel and use quick release.

4 Add tofu, bell pepper and green beans to pot. Secure lid and move pressure release valve to Sealing position. Press Pressure Cook or Manual; cook at low pressure 1 minute.

5 When cooking is complete, press Cancel and use quick release. Stir in basil and lime juice. Serve with rice, if desired.

Colcannon

Makes 6 to 8 servings

4 slices bacon, chopped

3 pounds russet potatoes, peeled and cut into 1-inch pieces

2 medium leeks, halved lengthwise and thinly sliced

½ cup water

1¼ teaspoons salt

¼ teaspoon black pepper

1 cup milk, divided

2 tablespoons butter, cut into pieces

½ small head savoy cabbage (about 1 pound), cored and thinly sliced (about 4 cups)

1 Press Sauté; cook and stir bacon in Instant Pot until crisp. Remove to paper towel-lined plate. Add potatoes, leeks, water, salt and pepper to pot; mix well.

2 Secure lid and move pressure release valve to Sealing position. Press Pressure Cook or Manual; cook at high pressure 5 minutes.

3 When cooking is complete, press Cancel and use quick release.

4 Press Sauté; add ½ cup milk and butter to pot. Cook and stir 1 minute, mashing potatoes until still slightly chunky. Add remaining ½ cup milk and cabbage; cook and stir 2 to 3 minutes or until cabbage is wilted. Stir in bacon.

Brussels Sprouts in Orange Sauce

Makes 4 servings

½ cup plus 2 tablespoons
    orange juice, divided

½ teaspoon salt

¼ teaspoon red pepper flakes

¼ teaspoon ground cinnamon

¼ teaspoon black pepper

8 ounces fresh brussels
    sprouts (about 3 cups)

2 teaspoons cornstarch

1 teaspoon honey

1 teaspoon shredded or
    grated orange peel

1 Combine ½ cup orange juice, salt, red pepper flakes, cinnamon and black pepper in Instant Pot; mix well. Stir in brussels sprouts.

2 Secure lid and move pressure release valve to Sealing position. Press Pressure Cook or Manual; cook at high pressure 2 minutes.

3 When cooking is complete, press Cancel and use quick release. Remove brussels sprouts to medium bowl with slotted spoon.

4 Stir remaining 2 tablespoons orange juice into cornstarch in small bowl until smooth. Press Sauté; add honey, orange peel and cornstarch mixture to pot. Cook 1 to 2 minutes or until sauce thickens, stirring constantly.

5 Pour sauce over brussels sprouts; stir gently to coat.

Mexican Corn Bread Pudding

Makes 8 servings

1 can (14¾ ounces)
   cream-style corn

¾ cup yellow cornmeal

2 eggs

1 can (4 ounces) diced
   green chiles

2 tablespoons vegetable oil

2 tablespoons sugar

2 teaspoons baking powder

¾ teaspoon salt

1¼ cups water

½ cup (2 ounces) shredded
   Cheddar cheese

1 Spray 6- to 7-inch (1½-quart) soufflé dish or round baking dish that fits inside Instant Pot with nonstick cooking spray.

2 Combine corn, cornmeal, eggs, chiles, oil, sugar, baking powder and salt in medium bowl; mix well. Pour into prepared dish. Cover dish tightly with foil.

3 Pour water into pot. Place rack in pot; place soufflé dish on rack.

4 Secure lid and move pressure release valve to Sealing position. Press Pressure Cook or Manual; cook at high pressure 25 minutes.

5 When cooking is complete, use natural release for 10 minutes, then release remaining pressure. Uncover; sprinkle with cheese. Tent with foil; let stand 5 minutes or until cheese is melted.

Curried Cauliflower and Potatoes

Makes 6 servings

3 tablespoons vegetable oil

1 medium onion, chopped

1 tablespoon minced garlic

1 tablespoon curry powder

1½ teaspoons salt

1½ teaspoons grated fresh ginger

1 teaspoon ground turmeric

1 teaspoon yellow or brown mustard seeds

¼ teaspoon red pepper flakes

½ cup water

1 medium head cauliflower, cut into 1-inch pieces

1½ pounds fingerling potatoes, cut into halves

1 Press Sauté; heat oil in Instant Pot. Add onion; cook and stir about 6 minutes or until beginning to brown. Add garlic, curry powder, salt, ginger, turmeric, mustard seeds and red pepper flakes; cook and stir 1 minute.

2 Stir in water, scraping up browned bits from bottom of pot. Stir in cauliflower and potatoes; mix well.

3 Secure lid and move pressure release valve to Sealing position. Press Pressure Cook or Manual; cook at high pressure 4 minutes.

4 When cooking is complete, press Cancel and use quick release.

DESSERTS

Chocolate Orange Bread Pudding

Makes 6 to 8 servings

4 ounces French baguette, cubed (about 4 cups)

¼ cup sugar

3 tablespoons unsweetened cocoa powder

1½ cups milk

3 eggs, lightly beaten

2 teaspoons grated orange peel

1 teaspoon vanilla

¾ teaspoon ground cinnamon

¼ teaspoon salt

1¼ cups water

¼ cup hot fudge topping

Maraschino cherries (optional)

1 Spray 6- to 7-inch (1½-quart) soufflé dish or round baking dish that fits inside Instant Pot with nonstick cooking spray. Place bread cubes in prepared dish.

2 Combine sugar and cocoa in medium bowl; mix well. Whisk in milk, eggs, orange peel, vanilla, cinnamon and salt until well blended. Pour mixture evenly over bread cubes. Cover dish tightly with foil.

3 Pour water into pot. Place soufflé dish on rack; lower rack into pot.

4 Secure lid and move pressure release valve to Sealing position. Press Pressure Cook or Manual; cook at high pressure 30 minutes.

5 When cooking is complete, use natural release for 10 minutes, then release remaining pressure.

6 Remove soufflé dish from pot. Remove foil; cool 5 to 10 minutes. Serve warm with hot fudge topping; garnish with cherries.

Applesauce Custard

Makes 6 servings

1½ cups unsweetened applesauce

½ teaspoon ground cinnamon

¼ teaspoon salt

4 eggs, at room temperature

½ cup half-and-half

¼ cup unsweetened apple juice concentrate

⅛ teaspoon ground nutmeg

1¼ cups water

1 Combine applesauce, cinnamon and salt in medium bowl; mix well. Whisk in eggs, half-and-half and apple juice concentrate until well blended. Pour into 6- to 7-inch (1½-quart) soufflé dish or round baking dish that fits inside Instant Pot. Sprinkle with nutmeg. Cover dish tightly with foil.

2 Pour water into pot. Place soufflé dish on rack; lower rack into pot.

3 Secure lid and move pressure release valve to Sealing position. Press Pressure Cook or Manual; cook at high pressure 30 minutes.

4 When cooking is complete, use natural release for 10 minutes, then release remaining pressure.

5 Remove soufflé dish from pot. Remove foil; cool to room temperature. Serve custard at room temperature or chilled.

Chocolate Rice Pudding

Makes 6 servings

1 cup water

1 cup uncooked long grain rice

½ teaspoon salt, divided

1½ cups milk

½ cup sugar

2 tablespoons cornstarch

½ teaspoon vanilla

½ cup semisweet chocolate chips

Whipped cream (optional)

Chocolate curls (optional)

1 Combine water, rice and ¼ teaspoon salt in Instant Pot; mix well.

2 Secure lid and move pressure release valve to Sealing position. Press Pressure Cook or Manual; cook at high pressure 4 minutes.

3 When cooking is complete, use natural release for 10 minutes, then release remaining pressure.

4 Whisk milk, sugar, cornstarch, vanilla and remaining ¼ teaspoon salt in medium bowl until well blended. Stir into cooked rice.

5 Press Sauté; cook and stir 5 minutes. Add chocolate chips; stir until melted and smooth. Top with whipped cream and chocolate curls, if desired.

Pumpkin Bread Pudding

Makes 4 servings

1 cup whole milk

2 eggs

½ cup canned pumpkin

⅓ cup packed brown sugar

1 tablespoon butter, melted

1½ teaspoons ground cinnamon

1 teaspoon vanilla

¼ teaspoon salt

¼ teaspoon ground nutmeg

8 slices cinnamon raisin bread, torn into small pieces (about 4 cups)

1¼ cups water

Bourbon Caramel Sauce (recipe follows, optional)

1 Spray 6- to 7-inch (1½-quart) soufflé dish or round baking dish that fits inside Instant Pot with nonstick cooking spray. Whisk milk, eggs, pumpkin, brown sugar, butter, cinnamon, vanilla, salt and nutmeg in large bowl until well blended. Add bread cubes; toss to coat. Pour into prepared dish; cover tightly with foil.

2 Pour water into pot. Place soufflé dish on rack; lower rack into pot.

3 Secure lid and move pressure release valve to Sealing position. Press Pressure Cook or Manual; cook at high pressure 40 minutes.

4 When cooking is complete, use natural release for 10 minutes, then release remaining pressure.

5 Remove soufflé dish from pot. Remove foil; cool 15 minutes. Meanwhile, prepare Bourbon Caramel Sauce, if desired. Serve bread pudding warm with sauce.

Bourbon Caramel Sauce

Combine ¼ cup (½ stick) butter, ¼ cup packed brown sugar and ¼ cup whipping cream in small saucepan; bring to a boil over high heat, stirring frequently. Remove from heat; stir in 1 tablespoon bourbon.

Warm Chocolate Cakes

Makes 4 servings

½ cup (1 stick) butter, cut into pieces

4 ounces bittersweet chocolate, chopped

½ teaspoon espresso powder or instant coffee granules

1 cup powdered sugar, plus additional for garnish

2 eggs

2 egg yolks

1 teaspoon vanilla

⅓ cup all-purpose flour

¼ teaspoon salt

1 cup water

1 Combine butter, chocolate and espresso powder in small saucepan; heat over very low heat until mixture is melted and smooth, stirring frequently. Whisk in 1 cup powdered sugar until well blended. Add eggs, egg yolks and vanilla; whisk until blended. Add flour and salt; whisk until blended. Divide batter among four 6-ounce ramekins or custard cups.

2 Pour water into Instant Pot; place rack in pot. Arrange ramekins on rack, stacking as necessary.

3 Secure lid and move pressure release valve to Sealing position. Press Pressure Cook or Manual; cook at high pressure 9 minutes.

4 When cooking is complete, press Cancel and use quick release.

5 Remove ramekins from pot. Gently dab paper towel over tops of cakes to remove any condensation. Sprinkle with additional powdered sugar; serve warm.

Plum Bread Pudding

Makes 6 servings

6 cups cubed brioche, egg bread or challah (1-inch cubes)

1½ tablespoons butter

2 large plums, pitted and cut into thin wedges

⅓ cup plus ½ tablespoon sugar, divided

3 eggs

¾ cup half-and-half

½ cup milk

½ teaspoon vanilla

¼ teaspoon salt

¼ teaspoon ground cinnamon

1¼ cups water

Whipping cream or vanilla ice cream (optional)

1 Preheat oven to 400°F. Spray 6- to 7-inch (1½-quart) soufflé dish or round baking dish that fits inside Instant Pot with nonstick cooking spray.

2 Spread bread cubes in single layer on ungreased baking sheet. Bake 6 to 7 minutes or until lightly toasted, stirring halfway through baking time.

3 Meanwhile, melt butter in large skillet over medium-high heat. Add plums and ½ tablespoon sugar; cook 2 minutes or until plums are softened and release juices. Beat eggs in large bowl. Add half-and-half, milk, remaining ⅓ cup sugar, vanilla, salt and cinnamon; mix well. Add plums and toasted bread cubes; stir gently to coat. Pour into prepared soufflé dish. Cover dish tightly with foil.

4 Pour water into pot. Place soufflé dish on rack; lower rack into pot.

5 Secure lid and move pressure release valve to Sealing position. Press Pressure Cook or Manual; cook at high pressure 35 minutes. When cooking is complete, use natural release for 10 minutes, then release remaining pressure.

6 Remove soufflé dish from pot. Let stand, covered, 15 minutes. Remove foil; serve warm with cream, if desired.

Rich Chocolate Pudding

Makes 6 servings

1½ cups whipping cream

4 ounces bittersweet chocolate, chopped

4 egg yolks

⅓ cup packed brown sugar

1 tablespoon unsweetened cocoa powder

1 teaspoon vanilla

¼ teaspoon salt

1¼ cups water

1 Heat cream to a simmer in medium saucepan over medium heat. Remove from heat. Add chocolate; stir until chocolate is melted and mixture is smooth.

2 Whisk egg yolks, brown sugar, cocoa, vanilla and salt in large bowl until well blended. Gradually add warm chocolate mixture, whisking constantly until blended. Strain into 6- to 7-inch (1½-quart) soufflé dish or round baking dish that fits inside Instant Pot. Cover tightly with foil.

3 Pour water into pot. Place soufflé dish on rack; lower rack into pot.

4 Secure lid and move pressure release valve to Sealing position. Press Pressure Cook or Manual; cook at low pressure 22 minutes.

5 When cooking is complete, use natural release for 5 minutes, then release remaining pressure.

6 Remove soufflé dish from pot. Remove foil; cool to room temperature. Cover and refrigerate at least 3 hours or up to 2 days.

Southern Sweet Potato Custard

Makes 4 servings

1 can (16 ounces) cut sweet potatoes, drained

1 can (12 ounces) evaporated milk, divided

½ cup packed brown sugar

2 eggs, lightly beaten

1 teaspoon ground cinnamon

½ teaspoon ground ginger

¼ teaspoon salt

1¼ cups water

Whipped cream (optional)

Ground nutmeg (optional)

1 Combine sweet potatoes and ¼ cup evaporated milk in food processor or blender; process until smooth. Add remaining milk, brown sugar, eggs, cinnamon, ginger and salt; process until well blended. Pour into 6- to 7-inch (1½-quart) soufflé dish or round baking dish that fits inside Instant Pot. Cover dish tightly with foil.

2 Pour water into pot. Place soufflé dish on rack; lower rack into pot.

3 Secure lid and move pressure release valve to Sealing position. Press Pressure Cook or Manual; cook at high pressure 40 minutes.

4 When cooking is complete, use natural release for 10 minutes, then release remaining pressure. Uncover; let stand 30 minutes.

5 Remove soufflé dish from pot. Remove foil; cool 30 minutes. Garnish with whipped cream and nutmeg.

Chocolate Cheesecake

Makes 1 (9-inch) cheesecake

22 chocolate sandwich
   cookies

¼ cup (½ stick) butter, melted

¼ cup seedless raspberry jam

3 tablespoons whipping
   cream

1 teaspoon instant coffee
   granules or espresso
   powder (optional)

½ cup semisweet chocolate
   chips *or* 3 ounces
   chopped bittersweet
   chocolate

1½ packages (8 ounces each)
   cream cheese, softened

½ cup sugar

2 eggs

½ teaspoon vanilla

1¼ cups water

   Whipped cream and fresh
   raspberries (optional)

1 Wrap outside of 7-inch springform pan with heavy-duty foil. Place cookies in food processor; process until finely ground. With motor running, drizzle in butter; process until well blended. Press mixture firmly on bottom of prepared pan. Spread jam over crust. Refrigerate crust while preparing filling.

2 Heat cream and coffee granules, if desired, in small saucepan until bubbles form around edge of pan. Remove from heat; add chocolate and let stand 2 minutes. Stir until well blended and smooth. Cool slightly.

3 Beat cream cheese in large bowl with electric mixer at medium-high speed until smooth. Add sugar; beat until light and fluffy. Add eggs, one at a time, beating well after each addition. Add vanilla and melted chocolate mixture; beat at low speed just until blended. Spread in prepared crust. (Pan should not be filled higher than ½ inch from top.) Cover pan tightly with foil.

4 Pour water into Instant Pot. Place pan on rack; lower rack into pot. Secure lid and move pressure release valve to Sealing position. Press Pressure Cook or Manual; cook at high pressure 45 minutes.

5 When cooking is complete, press Cancel and use quick release. Remove pan from pot. Remove foil; cool 1 hour. Run thin knife around edge of cheesecake to loosen (do not remove side of pan). Refrigerate 2 to 3 hours or overnight.

6 Remove side of pan. Garnish with whipped cream and raspberries.

Apple Spice Bread Pudding

Makes 4 servings

4 eggs

1 can (5 ounces) evaporated milk

½ cup packed brown sugar

¼ cup apple cider or apple juice

1 teaspoon ground cinnamon

½ teaspoon vanilla

¼ teaspoon salt

¼ teaspoon ground nutmeg

¼ teaspoon ground allspice

4 cups bread cubes

1½ cups cubed peeled Granny Smith apples (about 2 small)

½ cup chopped pecans

1¼ cups water

Ice cream (optional)

Caramel topping (optional)

1 Spray 6- to 7-inch (1½-quart) soufflé dish or round baking dish that fits inside Instant Pot with nonstick cooking spray.

2 Whisk eggs, evaporated milk, brown sugar, apple cider, cinnamon, vanilla, salt, nutmeg and allspice in large bowl until well blended. Add bread cubes, apples and pecans; toss to coat. Pour into prepared dish; cover tightly with foil.

3 Pour water into pot. Place soufflé dish on rack; lower rack into pot.

4 Secure lid and move pressure release valve to Sealing position. Press Pressure Cook or Manual; cook at high pressure 40 minutes.

5 When cooking is complete, use natural release for 10 minutes, then release remaining pressure. Remove soufflé dish from pot. Remove foil; serve warm with ice cream and caramel topping, if desired.

Poached Autumn Fruit

Makes 4 to 6 servings

1 orange, peeled and halved
2½ to 3 cups water
½ cup dried cranberries
¼ cup sugar
2 tablespoons honey
1 teaspoon vanilla
1 whole cinnamon stick
2 Granny Smith apples,
    peeled and halved
2 Bartlett pears, peeled
    and quartered
Vanilla ice cream (optional)

1 Squeeze juice from orange halves into Instant Pot; place orange halves in pot. Add 2½ cups water, cranberries, sugar, honey, vanilla and cinnamon stick; mix well. Add apples and pears; stir to coat. (Liquid should just cover fruit; if fruit is not covered, add additional water to cover.)

2 Secure lid and move pressure release valve to Sealing position. Press Pressure Cook or Manual; cook at high pressure 1 minute.

3 When cooking is complete, press Cancel and use quick release. Remove apples, pears and cranberries to plate with slotted spoon; let stand until cool enough to handle.

4 Meanwhile, press Sauté; cook about 10 minutes or until liquid is reduced by one third and thickens slightly. Discard orange halves and cinnamon stick. Pour liquid through fine-mesh strainer into medium bowl; return to pot.

5 Cut apple and pears into 1-inch pieces. Add to pot; stir gently to coat. Serve with vanilla ice cream, if desired.

Fudgy Chocolate Pudding Cake

Makes 6 servings

¾ cup plus ⅓ cup granulated sugar, divided

1 cup all-purpose flour

¼ cup plus 3 tablespoons unsweetened cocoa powder, divided

2 teaspoons baking powder

¼ teaspoon salt

½ cup milk

⅓ cup butter, melted

1 teaspoon vanilla

½ cup packed brown sugar

1 cup hot water

1¼ cups water

Vanilla ice cream (optional)

1 Spray 6- to 7-inch (1½-quart) soufflé dish or round baking dish that fits inside Instant Pot with nonstick cooking spray.

2 Combine ¾ cup granulated sugar, flour, ¼ cup cocoa, baking powder and salt in medium bowl; mix well. Add milk, butter and vanilla; whisk until well blended. Spread batter in prepared soufflé dish; smooth top. Combine brown sugar, remaining ⅓ cup granulated sugar and 3 tablespoons cocoa in small bowl; mix well. Sprinkle evenly over batter. Pour 1 cup hot water over top. (Do not stir.)

3 Pour 1¼ cups water into pot. Place soufflé dish on rack; lower rack into pot.

4 Secure lid and move pressure release valve to Sealing position. Press Pressure Cook or Manual; cook at high pressure 40 minutes.

5 When cooking is complete, use natural release for 10 minutes, then release remaining pressure.

6 Remove soufflé dish from pot; let stand 5 minutes. Serve warm with ice cream, if desired.

PRESSURE COOKING TIMES

MEAT

MEAT	MINUTES UNDER PRESSURE	PRESSURE	RELEASE
Beef, Bone-in Short Ribs	35 to 45	High	Natural
Beef, Brisket	60 to 75	High	Natural
Beef, Ground	8	High	Natural
Beef, Roast (round, rump or shoulder)	60 to 70	High	Natural
Beef, Stew Meat	20 to 25	High	Natural or Quick
Lamb, Chops	5 to 10	High	Quick
Lamb, Leg or Shanks	35 to 40	High	Natural
Lamb, Stew Meat	12 to 15	High	Quick
Pork, Baby Back Ribs	25 to 30	High	Natural
Pork, Chops	7 to 10	High	Quick
Pork, Ground	5	High	Quick
Pork, Loin	15 to 25	High	Natural
Pork, Shoulder or Butt	45 to 60	High	Natural
Pork, Stew Meat	15 to 20	High	Quick

POULTRY

POULTRY	MINUTES UNDER PRESSURE	PRESSURE	RELEASE
Chicken Breasts, Bone-in	7 to 10	High	Quick
Chicken Breasts, Boneless	5 to 8	High	Quick
Chicken Thigh, Bone-in	10 to 14	High	Natural
Chicken Thigh, Boneless	8 to 10	High	Natural
Chicken Wings	10 to 12	High	Quick

Chicken, Whole	22 to 26	High	Natural
Eggs, Hard-Cooked (3 to 12)	9	Low	Quick
Turkey Breast, Bone-in	25 to 30	High	Natural
Turkey Breast, Boneless	15 to 20	High	Natural
Turkey Legs	35 to 40	High	Natural
Turkey, Ground	8 to 10	High	Quick

SEAFOOD

SEAFOOD	MINUTES UNDER PRESSURE	PRESSURE	RELEASE
Cod	2 to 3	Low	Quick
Crab	2 to 3	Low	Quick
Halibut	6	Low	Quick
Mussels	1 to 2	Low	Quick
Salmon	4 to 5	Low	Quick
Scallops	1	Low	Quick
Shrimp	2 to 3	Low	Quick
Swordfish	4 to 5	Low	Quick
Tilapia	3	Low	Quick

DRIED BEANS AND LEGUMES

DRIED BEANS AND LEGUMES	UNSOAKED	SOAKED	PRESSURE	RELEASE
Black Beans	22 to 25	8 to 10	High	Natural
Black-Eyed Peas	9 to 11	3 to 5	High	Natural
Cannellini Beans	30 to 35	8 to 10	High	Natural
Chickpeas	35 to 40	18 to 22	High	Natural
Great Northern Beans	25 to 30	7 to 10	High	Natural

Kidney Beans	20 to 25	8 to 12	High	Natural
Lentils, Brown or Green	10 to 12	n/a	High	Natural
Lentils, Red or Yellow Split	1	n/a	High	Natural
Navy Beans	20 to 25	7 to 8	High	Natural
Pinto Beans	22 to 25	8 to 10	High	Natural
Split Peas	8 to 10	n/a	High	Natural

GRAINS

	LIQUID PER CUP	MINUTES UNDER PRESSURE	PRESSURE	RELEASE
Barley, Pearled	2	18 to 22	High	Natural
Barley, Whole	2½	30 to 35	High	Natural
Bulgur	3	8	High	Natural
Farro	2	10 to 12	High	Natural
Grits, Medium	4	12 to 15	High	10 minute natural
Millet	1½	1	High	Natural
Oats, Rolled	2	4 to 5	High	10 minute natural
Oats, Steel-Cut	3	10 to 13	High	10 minute natural
Quinoa	1½	1	High	10 minute natural
Polenta, Instant	3	5	High	5 minute natural
Rice, Arborio	2	6 to 7	High	Quick
Rice, Brown	1	22	High	10 minute natural
Rice, White Long Grain	1	4	High	10 minute natural

VEGETABLES

	MINUTES UNDER PRESSURE	PRESSURE	RELEASE
Artichokes, Whole	9 to 12	High	Natural
Beets, Medium Whole	18 to 24	High	Quick
Brussels Sprouts, Whole	2 to 3	High	Quick

Cabbage, Sliced	3 to 5	High	Quick
Carrots, Sliced	2 to 4	High	Quick
Cauliflower, Florets	2 to 3	High	Quick
Cauliflower, Whole	3 to 5	High	Quick
Corn on the Cob	2 to 4	High	Quick
Eggplant	3 to 4	High	Quick
Fennel, Sliced	3 to 4	High	Quick
Green Beans	2 to 4	High	Quick
Kale	3	High	Quick
Leeks	3	High	Quick
Okra	3	High	Quick
Potatoes, Baby or Fingerling	6 to 10	High	Natural
Potatoes, New	7 to 9	High	Natural
Potatoes, 1-inch pieces	4 to 6	High	Quick
Potatoes, Sweet, 1-inch pieces	3	High	Quick
Potatoes, Sweet, Whole	8 to 12	High	Natural
Spinach	1	High	Quick
Squash, Acorn, Halved	7	High	Natural
Squash, Butternut, 1-inch pieces	4 to 6	High	Quick
Squash, Spaghetti, Halved	6 to 10	High	Natural
Tomatoes, cut into pieces for sauce	5	High	Natural

METRIC CONVERSION CHART

VOLUME MEASUREMENTS (dry)

1/8 teaspoon = 0.5 mL
1/4 teaspoon = 1 mL
1/2 teaspoon = 2 mL
3/4 teaspoon = 4 mL
1 teaspoon = 5 mL
1 tablespoon = 15 mL
2 tablespoons = 30 mL
1/4 cup = 60 mL
1/3 cup = 75 mL
1/2 cup = 125 mL
2/3 cup = 150 mL
3/4 cup = 175 mL
1 cup = 250 mL
2 cups = 1 pint = 500 mL
3 cups = 750 mL
4 cups = 1 quart = 1 L

VOLUME MEASUREMENTS (fluid)

1 fluid ounce (2 tablespoons) = 30 mL
4 fluid ounces (1/2 cup) = 125 mL
8 fluid ounces (1 cup) = 250 mL
12 fluid ounces (1 1/2 cups) = 375 mL
16 fluid ounces (2 cups) = 500 mL

WEIGHTS (mass)

1/2 ounce = 15 g
1 ounce = 30 g
3 ounces = 90 g
4 ounces = 120 g
8 ounces = 225 g
10 ounces = 285 g
12 ounces = 360 g
16 ounces = 1 pound = 450 g

DIMENSIONS

1/16 inch = 2 mm
1/8 inch = 3 mm
1/4 inch = 6 mm
1/2 inch = 1.5 cm
3/4 inch = 2 cm
1 inch = 2.5 cm

OVEN TEMPERATURES

250°F = 120°C
275°F = 140°C
300°F = 150°C
325°F = 160°C
350°F = 180°C
375°F = 190°C
400°F = 200°C
425°F = 220°C
450°F = 230°C

BAKING PAN SIZES

Utensil	Size in Inches/Quarts	Metric Volume	Size in Centimeters
Baking or	8×8×2	2 L	20×20×5
Cake Pan	9×9×2	2.5 L	23×23×5
(square or	12×8×2	3 L	30×20×5
rectangular)	13×9×2	3.5 L	33×23×5
Loaf Pan	8×4×3	1.5 L	20×10×7
	9×5×3	2 L	23×13×7
Round Layer	8×1½	1.2 L	20×4
Cake Pan	9×1½	1.5 L	23×4
Pie Plate	8×1¼	750 mL	20×3
	9×1¼	1 L	23×3
Baking Dish	1 quart	1 L	—
or Casserole	1½ quart	1.5 L	—
	2 quart	2 L	—